FISHING
SALTWATER
BAITS

FISHING SALTWATER BAITS

ERIC BURNLEY

BURFORD BOOKS

Printed in the United States of America.

10   9   8   7   6   5   4   3   2   1

Library of Congress Cataloging-in-Publication Data
    Burnley, Eric B.
    Fishing saltwater baits / Eric Burnley.
            p.   cm.
    Includes index.
    ISBN 978-1-58080-157-7
    1. Saltwater fishing—Equipment and supplies.   2. Fishing baits.   I. Title.

SH457.B85 2009
799.16—dc22

                                                                    2009009359

CONTENTS

DEDICATION

This book is dedicated to Daria Marie Burnley with the hope that she will grow up to be a much better fisherman than her father, her uncle and her grandfather.

Acknowledgments

I have been fishing for a very long time and must thank everyone who helped me along the way because I have learned something from them all. Mrs. Cora Eppler showed me how to bend a pin into a fish hook, tie the hook to a stick with a length of black linen line and bait the hook with a white-bread dough ball. Who knew then that my first fish would be the start of a life-long career and passion?

Pete Barrett must accept some of the blame for purchasing the first article I wrote, and Rip Cunningham followed along by buying my first work in *Salt Water Sportsman*. All the research that went into 35 years of writing went into this book.

While I have been writing for a long time I have been reading much longer, including articles in *Field and Stream* by Robert Ruark and the *Salt Water Sportsman* articles by Al Ristori, not to mention the hundreds of articles in *The Fisherman* Magazine that I read and edited. It would be impossible not to learn something from all that expertise.

My personal thanks goes to my sons Ric and Roger who helped me by posing for photos and keeping me up to date on the latest fishing techniques. No father could ask for better children.

The Fishing Encyclopedia by Ken Schultz was by my side during the writing of this book. There was never a question this book could not answer.

Finally I must thank my wife Barbara who had to put up with me not only while I was writing this book, but for the past 42 years.

Introduction

Fishermen employed bait long before tying the first fly or carving out the first lure. Primitive tribes fashioned fish hooks out of bone and there is a reference to fishing with bait from the earliest civilizations in the Middle East. Even the great fly fishing icon Izaak Walton used various baits in his pursuit of trout.

In today's fishing environment bait is an important tool for the inshore angler after spot or summer flounder as well as for the offshore adventurer looking for marlin or tuna. Patrons of the high surf may dream about catching that 50-pound striper on a carefully carved wood plug, but will stand a much better chance of achieving the 50-pound mark by soaking a chunk of bunker, a whole quahaug or casting a live eel.

Some in the angling community look upon bait fishing the way a gourmet looks at a hot dog. These elitists would never soil their hands with a gooey clam or dig in the mud for a bloodworm. While I do respect their right to choose the technique that best suits their fishing objectives, I feel they miss out on a lot of fun when the big weakfish are only hitting live spot or the croaker are taking squid in 80 feet of water.

The objective of this book is to educate the saltwater angler on all aspects of bait fishing, from acquiring the bait to the proper presentation. We will examine hooks, lines and rigs in an attempt to produce the most efficient setup for catching fish with bait. Proper care to keep the bait fresh or alive will be covered, including the construction of various storage containers. We will also consider the manufactured bait products that have become popular during the past few years.

Anglers who enjoy sitting on old lawn furniture alongside a tidal creek soaking bloodworms for white perch, as well as those who troll rigged ballyhoo behind multi-million dollar sportfishermen in an attempt to catch a big blue marlin, all have one thing in common: they fish with bait. Most of us fall somewhere in between these two extremes, and learning all we can about fishing with bait will make us more productive fishermen.

FISHING SALTWATER BAITS

1

FRESH BAIT

Fresh bait will always out-produce the frozen variety and should be the first choice of all anglers. Perhaps mullet are the preferred offering for bluefish in the fall, but the local tackle shop may only have bags of the frozen product. Ask what fresh baits are available and if the shop has spot or bunker, take those and leave the frozen mullet behind.

Most tackle shops turn over their fresh bait inventory long before it goes bad. When the supply exceeds the demand they would rather freeze any leftover bait for later sale then take a chance of ruining their reputation by offering a product that is past its sell-by date.

Even with this in mind, the prudent angler will always inspect the bait before purchase. It is disturbing to open a package of bait on the fishing grounds and discover that the contents are not of the quality expected. You can demand satisfaction from the seller after returning to the dock, but your trip is ruined.

Inspect bait for freshness first by smelling the fish. It should have a clean smell and not the odor associated with rotting flesh. The eyes should be clear and the gills red. The flesh should be firm when pressed with a finger, and bounce back to its original shape. The dealer must have the bait in a refrigerator or on ice in a cooler. Bait that has been allowed to soak in ice water will become soft very quickly.

There are occasions when the fresh bait you use is the small fish you catch. On deep water fishing trips grunts, bergalls and any number of other small fish may be caught. While not top table fare these fish may be cut into sections and sent back down to the bottom.

In the surf we often catch spot or pinfish. Once again the small fish is cut up and used as fresh bait. I have caught weakfish and blues on cut spot while others fishing nearby were content to keep catching spot on bloodworms. Once the bait is in your possession it is a good idea to treat the investment with care. Keep a cooler just for bait. This keeps the bait fresh and your lunch from adopting the flavor of bunker, mullet or whatever is the bait *du jour*. It is also never a good idea to keep the bait in the same cooler intended to hold your catch. Once a threshing fish hits the cooler all the bait will be scattered, crushed and otherwise ruined.

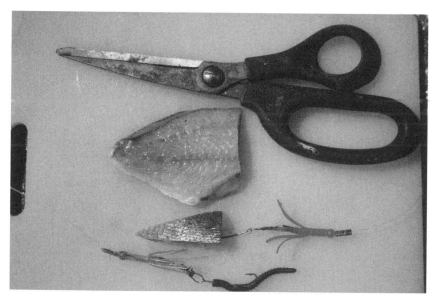

Cut spot and bloodworm on a surf rig.

When using cut bait, remove the number of whole fish needed from the bag or plastic container in the cooler, then return the remainder to the ice as soon as possible. Have a separate container for the cut bait, and keep it on ice as well. While it is a good idea to cut up enough bait for several rebaitings, it is a bad idea to let the extra pieces bake on the cutting board. Treat them well and they will do a much better job.

There are several forms of ice that may be used in a bait cooler. The most common form is bagged cubes poured on the bottom of the cooler with the bait containers placed on top of the ice. You can also purchase a device that fits in the cooler and separates the bait from the ice. These are especially popular on offshore fishing excursions when large numbers of pre-rigged baits must be stored. Wet newspapers will do an adequate job of keeping smaller amounts of bait from the ice while still transferring the cold to the bait.

Alternatives to bagged ice include frozen milk jugs of water, which are very popular because they can be reused and save money. The jugs must be secured in the cooler to prevent them from moving around and crushing the bait, or what begins as nice fresh bunker before the run to the fishing grounds may arrive as bunker chum. These jugs are also susceptible to forming small holes that allow the fresh water inside to leak and spoil the bait.

The small frozen ice packs are perfect for keeping a small amount of bait in a lunch-pail size cooler. One or two of these packs fit nicely on the bottom of the cooler with the bait on top. This is a very convenient way to carry bait on a head boat or a pier.

Small coolers are great when everyone on board a private boat is fishing with the same baits. Have containers such as soft butter tubs for each bait and set them directly on top of the ice packs. One container may hold shiners, another squid and a third live minnows in a small amount of water. Each angler will have a separate cooler, and when it is time to rebait he or she does not have to fish the minnows out of the live cart or open the main cooler for shiners and squid. This system is convenient and keeps the primary bait colder, since it does not have to be opened every time someone needs fresh bait.

At the end of the fishing day some fresh bait may be left over. To save it for another trip, give the bait a coating of kosher salt, put it in a resealable plastic bag and stick it in the freezer. The salt will keep the bait flexible and help preserve its color.

FoodSaver bags are another option for saving bait. These bags are airtight and bait will still be usable after a year in the freezer.

Fresh Shrimp

One bait that should never be used after it has been frozen is shrimp. Not only does freezing make the bait soft, it apparently has some effect on its appeal to the fish.

On one bright and sunny fall afternoon I was fishing from a pier in North Carolina, and catching nothing on my frozen shrimp while the couple next to me cranked in sea mullet (northern king-fish) on every cast using fresh shrimp. I had bypassed the fresh shrimp because it cost twice as much as the frozen product, a decision I came to regret. The lady finally offered me some fresh shrimp and I was able to put a few mullet in my cooler before the bite turned off. Never satisfied to take a lesson at face value, I tried frozen shrimp a few more times before I was convinced to shoot the lock off of my wallet and buy only the fresh variety.

Bait shops in the south carry fresh shrimp, while those in the north do not. I find the dividing line located between Virginia and North Carolina. Even where it is a staple, fresh shrimp may not be available every day. Weather conditions play an important role in the availability of fresh shrimp because if the shrimp boats can't sail there will be nothing in the bait box.

Expect to buy fresh shrimp in its natural state. The head will be attached along with all of the various appendages. It won't look like the shrimp at Red Lobster, but you are going to fish with it, not eat it. (Actually, I have been known to cook the leftover bait shrimp for a tasty appetizer).

Bait shrimp should be firm and not mushy. It should have a fresh smell and not be crushed by the net or the weight of other critters captured at the same time.

To rig fresh shrimp, I use long shanked Chestertown hooks that are run through the shrimp from the head to the tail. All hooks should be made from light wire, as shrimp is a delicate bait. Some anglers hook their shrimp through the hard shell on top of the animal's head. This is a solid perch for the hook, but it does not give a natural presentation. Running a hook through a shrimp makes the bait appear to be swimming in a normal manner and puts the barb in the tail, where a fish is most likely to attack.

RIGS FOR FRESH BAIT

The following rigs will work with any fresh bait, either cut in chunks or used whole.

Rig Materials

The materials used to tie rigs must be of high quality, but are not necessarily expensive. In most applications monofilament leader or fishing line will do the job. There will be times when the more expensive Fluorocarbon line is needed due to very clear water or leader-shy fish. In those cases do not skimp because of the cost—use the Fluorocarbon or you will pay with lost opportunities.

Hooks must be of the highest quality as well. Here the cost difference between the best and something less is hardly noticeable.

When tying my own rigs I use as little hardware as possible. Many store-bought rigs employ snaps or swivels where the running line is attached, and to hold the sinker. I use a perfection loop to connect the line to the rig and a double surgeon's loop to hold the sinker. I also use the double surgeon's loop to connect the hook to the rig, but will admit that the dropper loop is a stronger and better-looking knot. In most instances the size of the fish is much smaller than the pound-test of the line, so the knot strength is of little importance. The knot strength is measured as a percentage of the line strength. A 50% knot tied in 50-pound line will break at 25 pounds. This is more than enough to hold most bottom fish. It often helps to have a weak knot holding the sinker, as it will break and free the rest of the rig from a snag.

I construct the rig from fishing line rather than leader material when fishing for small species such as spot, croaker, snapper or whiting. These fish have little chance of breaking the 50-pound line I use, and working with line is much easier than trying to tie rigs with leader material. Once the size of the fish approaches (or could approach) five pounds, I go with the leader material. Leader material should also be used when fishing hard structure due to the

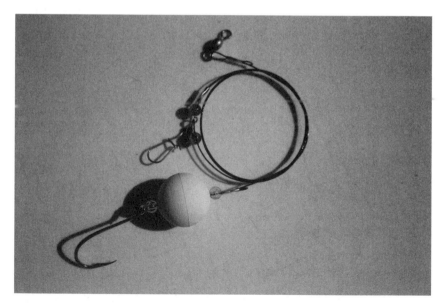

Surf rig for big blues. Note wire leader.

potential for abrasion. I will go as light as 20-pound material when fishing for summer flounder, and as heavy as 100-pound leader when cobia or big striped bass are the target. Once you require leader heavier than 100-pound, crimping should be used instead of tying knots.

Wire leaders are needed when toothy critters like king mackerel, bluefish and wahoo are the target. Wire leader comes in two forms, braided and single strand. Braided is easier to work with and is suitable for most inshore species. The single strand product is used for fishing offshore, when trolling is the normal technique. Both types are subject to kinking and the braided line will fray. The prudent angler will check the leader after every fish and replace leaders with even the slightest sign of wear.

Several years ago I was fishing the Outer Banks of North Carolina on a beautiful fall day. We were catching 15-pound bluefish using cut mullet and the action was constant. I checked my plastic-coated braided wire leader after catching a blue and found the slightest nick in the plastic coating. Since I was anxious to get back to the hot bite and the nick was small, I did not change the rig. As soon as the bait hit bottom, another big blue picked it up and when the line came tight the leader parted. My effort to save time cost me another fish—and even more time, as I had to crank in the line before retying.

Connectors such as snaps and swivels used to connect the running line to the rig are critical to success and must be of the highest quality. As with hooks, the cost between good and bad is not worth discussing. Duo-lock and coast-lock style snaps are very good. Inter-lock snaps are very weak and should not be used in salt water. Ball bearing swivels must be used when trolling to prevent line twist. Barrel swivels are fine when still fishing, and the small swivels available today are good when the leader must be cranked through the rod guides.

Top-Bottom Rig

I expect this is the most popular rig in use today. It is created in many forms and used for everything from spot to golden tilefish.

The basic top-bottom rig has one hook close to the sinker, and a second hook close to the connection of the rig to the running line. Tie a double surgeon's loop to the end of a three-foot section of 50-pound fishing line. This loop will hold the sinker. On the other end of the line tie a perfection loop to connect the rig to the running line. Between these two knots tie two loops using a double surgeon's or a dropper. The same procedure is used when tying the rig with leader material.

Attaching the hooks to the rig can be as simple as using a pair of snelled hooks looped through the two loops on the rig, or sliding the two loops through the eyes of the hooks for a more direct connection. I am fond of this latter method when fishing for tog, triggerfish or other known bait stealers. Having a very short leader between the hook and the rig allows the angler to detect even the slightest bite.

Another variation is to use a long leader on the bottom loop and a shorter one on the top. This setup is popular with summer flounder fishermen who believe the fish may see the first bait pass overhead and grab the second bait when it passes by. The longer leader also allows the bait to have more action as it flutters along.

Adding floats, feathers, spinners, beads and other decorations to the hooks is common. The added attractors can be important, especially when the water is murky.

Fish-Finder Rig

The fish-finder rig uses only one hook, along with a device that features a small cylinder through which the line passes and a snap for securing a sinker. This device allows the fish to take line without feeling the weight of the sinker, and may be made of plastic, leather or metal. The running line is passed through the fish-finder device

Ric Burnley with a triggerfish caught on a clam.

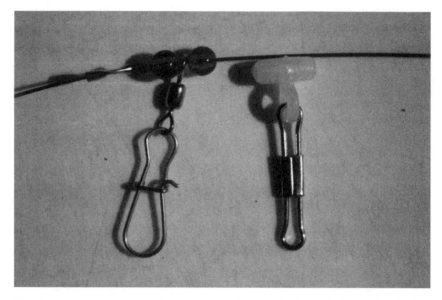

Fishfinder rig made with a swivel, snap, and red plastic beads on the left and a plastic model on the right.

and then secured to a swivel large enough to prevent the leader from passing back through the fishfinder. The hook is attached to the leader and the leader is then attached to the swivel on the end of the running line. When a fish picks up the bait, it can move off without resistance until the reel is engaged and the line comes tight.

Prior to the use of circle hooks, the angler had to crank out all the slack in the line, and when it came tight he had to set the hook. With a circle hook, once the line comes tight the fish will be hooked.

The length of the leader varies with the type of fishing. Surf fishermen keep the leader very short, less than 6 inches, because a long leader with a heavy bait becomes another weight, and casting two weights separated by two or three feet has a tendency to cut down on casting distance. The short leader keeps the two weights close and improves casting distance.

Fishing with live bait or chunks from a boat allows the angler to use a longer leader. I use 6 feet of 100-pound leader when soaking bunker for cobia and 3 feet of 50-pound when using live eels to target striped bass. Keep in mind that when the swivel hits the rod tip, the fish must be controlled by hand until it is landed. Too long a leader can cause the mate a considerable amount of trouble as he tries to bring the fish alongside.

Three-Way Swivel Rig

The three-way swivel rig is very similar to the fish-finder rig except that the line cannot play out when the fish picks up the bait. This rig works well when the angler wants to have more control of the bait, as in summer flounder fishing, when it is necessary to drop back to the fish once the pickup has occurred.

Three-way swivel rig.

With the three-way swivel rig a much longer leader may be used, and this allows the bait more freedom to move. I have used 30-foot leaders when wire line trolling for summer flounder and striped bass.

The three-way swivel rig begins with a three-way swivel, but I expect you already figured that out. Tie a 1- to 2-foot piece of 30- to 50-pound test fishing line to one eye of the swivel. I put surgeon's loops in either end of the line, using one to connect it to the swivel and the other to hold the sinker. Once again, the weak knot comes in handy should the sinker decide to take up permanent residence on the bottom.

The leader is attached to the three-way swivel with a clinch knot. As mentioned, the leader can be as long as you feel is necessary. In most still-fishing situations I find 3 to 6 feet is adequate. I use a circle hook with this rig and when the fish comes tight against the drag, he is hooked. This is the rig I use while soaking a bait on the bottom when chunking for striped bass or tuna.

Chum and Chunk Rigs

Chumming and chunking are very popular on the inshore and the offshore grounds. In the north bluefish, tuna, sharks and weakfish are targets of chummers and chunkers. Further south, snappers, king mackerel, cobia, bonito and just about everything that swims can be attracted with chum.

By filling the water with a strong scent of food and tempting the fish to gather close to the boat where the food is being dispersed, the angler can often catch numerous fish on relativity light tackle while remaining in one place.

The difference between chumming and chunking is the material placed in the water. Chum is ground-up fish mixed with some water to create a stinky mess that is ladled over the side. Chunking is done with small pieces of fish that are tossed overboard and sink through the water column. The chum and the chunks may be frozen, but the bait should always be fresh.

Bunker ready for the chum grinder.

In the Florida Keys mates mix shrimp, pilchards and other baits with wet sand to form chum balls. As the balls fall to the bottom, the bait is released and dispersed throughout the entire water column. A similar procedure is done in the north when grass shrimp are mixed with sand to attract weakfish.

Sometimes the chum and chunks may be from one type of fish while the bait is an entirely different species. Tuna fishermen may chunk with butterfish and put spearing on the hook. Shark fishermen often use bunker chum and then bait with mackerel or bluefish. When they are available, live bait such as spot or bunker may be drifted back in the chum or chunk line. Toss a handful of live or even dead peanut bunker in a tuna chunk line and watch the action. The reflection off their scales will set the tuna nuts.

Fishing a bait in a chum or chunk line is done using several methods. Allowing an unweighted hook to sink at the same rate as the chum or chunk is the most common technique. In situations

Grinding chum.

Bunker cut for chunking.

where the current is strong it may be necessary to add some weight to the line. This is usually accomplished with rubber core pinch-on sinkers. These weights are easy to change as conditions warrant.

The angler will play out the line to maintain slack, so the bait sinks without any restriction. Count the number of pulls, the distance from the reel to the first guide, so when a pickup is felt the angler will have some idea how many pulls away from the boat the fish are holding. With circle hooks, once the pickup is detected the angler only has to engage the reel and crank out the slack to hook the fish.

The second option is to drop a baited hook to the bottom on a fish-finder or three-way swivel rig. At this point the rod is placed in a holder and left there until a fish has the bait. With a fish-finder, engage the reel and the fish will be hooked when the line comes tight. A three-way swivel rig will hook the fish on its own and the screaming drag will notify the angler that his attention is required.

A five-gallon bucket of ground chum mixed with a little water.

Baiting a hook for this style of fishing has more options than a Cadillac. Bluefish chummers insist that the heart of a bunker is the prime bait, while tuna chunkers will play hide-the-hook when fishing with an entire butterfish.

When using baits from whole fish, it is important that they be cut in a shape that will not spin in the current. Triangles cut from filets in the shape of long pennants and hooked in the wide end are widely used. When a fast current is encountered, cutting wedges from the back of a bunker will reduce the water resistance of the bait while adding a bit of weight.

A unique device for bluefishing in a chum slick is the bluefish spinnerbait. It is constructed of solid wire with a spinner blade and some hair placed in a position to cover the hook. A strip of bait is placed on the hook, and the rig is allowed to drift back in the chum slick. The blade moves slowly and attracts the bluefish to the bait.

Using whole baits, like butterfish, requires placing the hook inside the fish and having the leader come out of the mouth. This is done by pulling the hook into the mouth and then pushing it through the gill opening and inside the body cavity. The leader exits out of the mouth and the target fish, usually tuna, does not see any hardware.

Chunking bluefish requires the use of a wire leader ahead of the hook. The leader does not have to be very long (six inches is usually enough), and making them out of single strand wire is the best method. Bend a Haywire twist in one end of the wire leader to form a loop and then secure the hook in the other end using the same method. Make 15 to 20 of these rigs before arriving on the bluefish grounds. Blues have a tendency to remain quite active when brought aboard the boat. It is much easier to unsnap the leader and drop the blue in the fish box then to try and unhook him on deck. Hooks may be removed back at the cleaning table or, if more rigs are required during the day, after the fish has expired in the cooler.

Ingredients for homemade chum. Bag of dried cat food, menhaden oil. Mix 1-cup oil with 2 gallons of cat food and just enough water to cover. Stir and let stand for half hour. Pour into plastic bags and freeze. Put frozen chum into onion bag and put the bag into the 5-gallon bucket. Chum will disperse through holes in bucket.

Fishing for sharks is a whole new subject. Most anglers chum with some sort of fish (bunker is popular), while setting out various baits at different depths and different distances from the boat. To accomplish this, the baited hooks are suspended from floats at various depths, with the deepest hook set furthest from the boat. It is a good idea to have one bait very close to the chum bucket, for that one shark that passes by all the other rigs in his quest to find the source of all that food.

Shark baits may be whole mackerel, squid or bluefish. Catch a blue and he can be quickly returned to the water as a live bait. The addition of a rubber skirt or other attractor ahead of the bait is common.

Shark rigs are usually 6 to 10 feet long and made from heavy mono and wire. The obvious danger to the leader is the shark's teeth, but sharks are also lost when they wrap up and kink a wire leader. Many anglers tie shark leaders in two sections. The hook is secured to either braided or single strand wire, and the wire is then mated to a longer mono leader with a swivel in between. The idea is to use the wire to keep the hook safe from bite offs, while the more flexible mono is able to withstand the shark's spinning and wrapping as he tries to escape.

Mooching Rig

Mooching is a technique using a fresh herring, with the head removed and the inside cleaned out. Used in the Northwest to catch salmon, the size of the bait depends on the size of the target fish. The angle of the cut determines the way the bait behaves in the water, with a slow roll being the most desirable effect.

The mooching rig consists of two or three snelled salmon hooks placed in the bait, with one in the front of the body cavity and the others behind the dorsal fin. The rig is then slow-trolled or drifted in areas of strong current. Often the captain will take the boat in and out of gear to maintain the correct trolling speed. Boat speed must also be adjusted to compensate for current speed during the course of the tide.

Mooching gear is a bit specialized. The rod may be 10½ feet long and the reel will hold several hundred yards of line. Levelwind reels are the most popular. Fly reels and shorter rods are used when smaller fish such as coho are the target.

To put the bait at the proper depth a keel sinker is used. The weight may be as much as 6 ounces. A barrel swivel is used above the sinker and the leader length is usually the same length as the rod.

While most of the time a trolled bait that spins is considered a bad thing, I have seen underwater photos of salmon mooching where the bait spins in a small circle. The salmon must consider this the normal activity for herring because they hit the bait without hesitation.

Kite Fishing

Fishing a fresh bait from a kite can be very effective. In the Florida Keys, they use flying fish rigged with the wings spread to tempt tuna and sailfish. The bait is sent aloft by the kite and skips across the surface in the manner of a flying fish. It hits the surface of one wave, then flies to the next one where a tuna is often waiting. This technique is labor-intensive, as the mate is responsible for keeping the bait flying and then cranking out the slack after the hit.

A special kite rod and reel are often used. The rod is very short and has the action of a pool cue. The reel is a fast-retrieve model used to bring in the kite line. The bait is on a standard rod and reel, so once it breaks free from the release clip the angler can enjoy the fight.

The fishing kites themselves are made especially for this application. They come in various weights to compensate for different wind conditions. Fishing a kite requires the captain to maintain a speed that along with the ambient wind will keep the kite flying. This can be a challenge on days with too much or not enough wind.

Kingfish Rig

The kingfish goes by many names, sea mullet, roundhead, whiting and king being the most common. There are two species of kingfish, northern and southern, and both have similar habits and appetites. Surf fishermen catch these fish more often than anglers fishing from boats, and shrimp are a prime bait.

Kingfish have small mouths located under their chins, making them very efficient bottom feeders. Shrimp compose a good part of their diet and thereby make an excellent bait.

Most anglers use a two-hook bottom rig for kings, and Chestertown hooks are the most popular armament.

I begin my king rig with a three-way swivel. I run the two-hook leader off one eye of the swivel and the sinker off the second eye on a very short leader. This keeps both hooks on the bottom where a king is most likely to find the bait. The addition of a few beads or spinner blades ahead of the hooks can help attract the kings, especially when the water is dirty. When conditions are reasonably calm I will use a bank sinker in the surf and keep the rig moving over the bottom until I find where the kings are feeding. When conditions are rough, the current will move the rig too fast for adequate control, so a more conventional surf sinker that will secure the rig is the best choice.

In the north where shrimp are not available, mole crabs (sand fleas) or bloodworms are the most popular kingfish baits.

Pompano Rig

Pompano are little jacks and can be very scrappy for their size. They are caught from the surf, bridges and boats. Their mouths are small, but they are not strictly bottom feeders.

My most successful encounter with pompano was in Florida, where we caught them over a sand bottom using shrimp on a small jig. They hit the bait well off the bottom, often almost as soon as it hit the water.

In the surf or from a bridge a jig baited with shrimp will also produce, but a two-hook bottom rig is more common. The majority of pompano bottom rigs employ floats above the hooks. The leaders to the hooks are short, making it easier to detect the bite.

2

LIVE BAIT

A properly presented live bait will fool even the wariest of fish. The key is to keep the bait alive and to use a rig that allows it to swim in a natural manner.

OBTAINING LIVE BAIT

Anglers have two choices when it comes to obtaining live bait. They can buy it or catch it. In recent years the cost of most live baits has become prohibitive for many fishermen. Adding to the problem is the loss of access to areas where live bait may be caught, as development has infringed upon marshland and small tidal creeks. Catching live bait is time consuming, and unless you have access to a safe location where the bait may be stored before use, the supply must be replenished before every trip.

Live bait can become very expensive fresh bait unless it is transported in a container that keeps it alive. Such a device must be available when the bait is being caught or purchased, as even a short drive to the marina or launch ramp without proper storage can prove fatal to most live baits.

On the West Coast live bait is used both as chum and as bait. The long range boats sailing from San Diego carry a considerable

Catching live bait can be fun.

Dolphin caught on live bait.

More than a mouthful.

amount of live bait and replenish their tanks during the trip. When fish are located, live bait is tossed over the side to attract them to the boat, and the angler will then cast a single bait into the action.

Catching big fish on a small bait requires special tackle. The rod must be able to cast a light bait and still have the brute power to handle a 200-pound tuna. The reel's line capacity has to be very large and the drag smooth as butter.

I have caught live spot and immediately turned them into live baits. Once I have one or two live bait rigs out, I will continue catching the spot and putting them in the live well. Head boats that travel to the Gulf Stream often have anglers who will live-line a fresh-caught grunt or small bluefish from the stern or top deck. This will produce king mackerel and dolphin, a nice addition to the day's catch.

MENHADEN, BUNKER, POGIES

These are three names for the same fish. They are found all along the Atlantic coast and are an important forage for almost every gamefish that swims.

Menhaden are caught in several ways. Gill nets and cast nets account for most of the menhaden used as live bait. It is also possible to snag this bait when gamefish have them packed into a tight school. The live bait is then allowed to swim just outside the school, making it an easy target.

Transporting menhaden requires a round bait tank that circulates large amounts of sea water. This type of tank must have a high-capacity pump to pull the water into the boat and an overflow to safely run the excess directly out of the tank and back overboard. Such systems are standard equipment on many new boats, while after-market kits are available in various sizes.

Live menhaden are sold from tackle shops in areas where king mackerel are a popular target. This is not an inexpensive operation, as the shop must pump a large amount of water to the holding tanks to keep the bait alive.

A peanut bunker.

During king mackerel tournaments, bait dealers will use a barge located in a convenient location for the tournament boats to stop by and purchase live menhaden before leaving the starting line. These barges can draw quite a crowd in the predawn darkness.

When menhaden cannot be purchased, they must be caught. Charter boats often set gill nets, and the party and crew pitch in to pull the net and get the bait to the livewell as soon as possible. Boats out of Hatteras Village, North Carolina work as a team and it is amazing to watch eight to ten 50- to 60-foot boats perform a water ballet as they set and pull nets in close proximity to each other.

Smaller trailered boats do not have the size to set a gill net, so they rely on cast nets. Many hard-core king mackerel fishermen will simply go home if they cannot catch a supply of menhaden. I am not that hard-core and will use live bluefish, spot or croaker that may be caught on bait or on a Sabiki rig.

A Sabiki rig is made using a light leader, with at least four and as many as ten dropper loops spaced six inches apart. Each dropper loop will hold a small hook decorated with a small feather, bead or other attractor. A sinker heavy enough to put the rig at the depth where the bait fish are located is tied to the end of the rig.

The rig is dropped down and jigged until as many baitfish as possible are hooked. Once the catch is in the boat it is placed in the live well or on ice as quickly as possible. Herring, shad, spot and croaker are all easy targets for a Sabiki rig.

In the northeast, live menhaden is a prime bait for striped bass. Anglers have no choice other than to catch their own bait, as tackle shops in this region do not carry live menhaden. Cast nets are used to catch a supply of menhaden; livewell and snag hooks are cast from boat or beach to hook a single bunker from a school. The bunker will then be pulled away from the safety of his companions and hopefully into the maw of a trophy striper.

Rigs for Menhaden

Live Menhaden Trolling Rig

Slow trolling a live menhaden is the most popular technique for catching trophy king mackerel. It is also effective on big cobia and the occasional tarpon. Amberjacks, crevalle jacks, sharks and even tuna will also hit a trolled menhaden. These larger fish are quite a challenge to land when snagged with a small treble.

A king mackerel rig is designed to snag the fish somewhere around the head rather than hook it in the mouth. Kings hit with a slashing strike that usually cuts the bait in half. No matter which end of the bait holds the hook, the king will hit the other end. By using two or three small trebles on a light wire leader the mackerel is more likely to find a hook. Even with three trebles adding up to nine hooks, a king can still take the bait without getting caught.

Kings can be very selective. While running a boat from the fly bridge I watched a king swim up next to a bunker, watch it for what seemed like an eternity, then simply fade back out of sight. On the other hand, I have seen kings jump 10 feet in the air and land right on top of a trolled menhaden.

King rigs are usually made from 40 to 60-pound braided wire leader. Some have a single hook and two trebles, some have three trebles and some have two trebles. When using a single hook it is placed in the head, and the two trebles are hooked in the back and the tail. The three-treble set up places one hook in the head, one in the body, and one is allowed to swing free near the tail. With the two-treble setup one is placed in the head, and one is hooked between the dorsal and the tail.

King rigs may be purchased or made. The pros who fish the king mackerel tournaments construct their own, while more casual king fishermen like me purchase their rigs at the local tackle shop.

Because it is important to keep the pressure light when trying to land a big king while using small trebles, the rods and reels designed for live bait trolling have a few special features. The rods have a soft tip to absorb the shock when a king makes a run. The reel must have a very smooth drag, as even the slightest bind could result in the loss of the fish. I personally prefer mono line when doing any kind of trolling because the stretch inherent in mono acts as an additional shock absorber.

In addition to running live baits off the stern and the outriggers, some anglers will hang a live menhaden from a kite. This is very effective, as the bait will often splash along just under the surface attracting kings from far and wide. When a fish hits a kite bait, a large amount of line falls in the water. This slack must be quickly cranked out to get the line tight and keep the fish hooked.

Snag Rig

The snag rig is a large treble hook that has a lead weight poured in the center. In Virginia these are known as Eastern Shore Mirro-O-

Lures. I am sure they have additional colloquial names in other parts of the country.

While frowned upon when used to snag gamefish, the snag rig can be very helpful when bunker are packed tight and stripers are patrolling the outside of the school. The angler will cast into the bunker, snag a bait and pull it outside the protection of the group with the hope that a striper will grab the obviously injured bait. This is done from the beach as well as from boats.

In my experience a big treble hook, as opposed to a snag rig, is not heavy enough to cast and does not sink fast enough to be effective. I have used an unweighted treble with a sinker or Stingsilver added to give it the necessary weight.

BLUEFISH

Live bluefish may be used in place of bunker. Be sure the area where you plan to fish does not have a minimum size limit on blues, as using too small a fish as bait could violate fishing regulations. Also be sure how many small bluefish you can accumulate as bait. Bluefish bag limits vary from 10 to 15, depending on the state.

Use a Sabiki rig to catch the small blues and keep them in the same type of livewell where you would keep menhaden. Fish them on the same rigs as you would bunker, and slow troll in the same manner.

Blues are hardier than bunker, but still require careful handling. Remove any dead fish from the livewell as soon as they are discovered, be it a bunker or a blue. Do not throw them overboard, as the dead ones can be cut up and thrown behind the boat as chum.

Snapper blues are a good bait for doormat flounder and tiderunner weakfish. They are hooked on a free-swimming rig (see below) and fished in locations where the big flounder or weaks are known to frequent. I like to place a circle hook through the eye sockets, while other fishermen will put the hook through the nose, mouth or just ahead of the dorsal fin.

HERRING

During the spring when herring run up the East Coast, they are closely followed by striped bass and bluefish. As you might expect, a live herring is an excellent bait at this time of year, but once again a large livewell is required.

Herring may be caught on hook and line or with a gill, cast, or dip net. Be sure to check local regulations before putting any kind of net in the water. Herring are somewhat delicate and a net can cause damage to many of the baits. Using shad darts or very small spoons is the most practical method for catching herring, but here too local fishing regulations must be obeyed. Delaware, for example, has a 10-fish limit on herring.

Herring are normally caught at spillways, where they gather because the dam keeps them from moving further upstream. Casting across the current and using a slow retrieve will locate any resident herring.

Because spillways are located quite a ways from the fishing grounds, a livewell must be installed in a truck to transport the bait to the sea. This is not an easy project and the salt water that will almost always get into the body of the truck will take years off the life of the vehicle. Nevertheless, I have seen everything from huge coolers to 55-gallon drums rigged up to keep herring alive during transport.

In a few cases a freshwater source will flow directly into the ocean. In this situation the herring will be close enough to the sea that a few may be caught at a time and used quickly. A small livewell mounted on the rod holder of a surf fishing vehicle will hold several herring.

Herring will show up at inlets as they begin their run up to freshwater. While the herring schools are seldom thick enough to snag or cast net, anglers may be able to hook some using shad darts or small spoons, and can immediately put the bait back overboard on a free-swimming rig.

Rigs for Herring

Free-Swiming Rig

When using any live bait, the idea is to make it as attractive as possible to the target fish. The free-swimming rig gives the baitfish as much freedom as it can have with a hook sticking in it while tied to a fishing line. I have seen some anglers cut off a fin or the tail of a bait to make it look hurt. I have never found this to be necessary.

The rig is simply a circle hook tied to a leader. The type and length of the leader will vary depending on the fish you are trying to catch. The leader is then connected to the running line with a snap or a snap swivel. My leaders are 3 to 4 feet long with a perfection knot in one end and the hook tied on the other end. The hook may be snelled or tied on with a clinch knot.

One situation in which the fish can be very leader-shy is live-lining for big striped bass. On many occasions, the leader will simply be the 20-pound test mono coming off the reel. Anything heavier and the bass will ignore the bait.

Fluorocarbon leader is supposed to disappear in the water, so it may be possible to go with a higher pound-test and still have a stealthy presentation. Another advantage of Fluorocarbon leader is its ability to resist abrasions. Leader material is much harder than fishing line and can take more abuse from rocks, shells and other nasty things found in the ocean.

There will be times when the fishing situation calls for getting the bait on a free-swimming rig down to the bottom. In shallow water with little current the bait will head for the bottom on its own. When fishing deeper water or when the current is strong, the addition of some weight to help the baitfish find bottom will be required. The rubber-core sinker is a good choice because it is easy to put on and take off. The sinker should be placed at least three feet above the bait. When even the largest rubber-core sinker is not heavy enough, use a fish-finder rig.

I always hook a live bait up from the bottom of the jaw and out the top. This keeps the bait alive, because it causes very little damage while allowing the fish to swim in a natural manner. All gamefish swallow a bait head–first, so having the hook in the mouth is a sure way to have the hook where you want it when the strike is made.

MUMMICHOG

The most prized bait in the northeast for flounder fishing is the mummichog (also called minnow, mud minnow, bull minnow, killie, or killfish). These are hardy little baits that can be kept alive on wet newspaper laid over ice in a cooler. More commonly they are kept in a minnow bucket that is placed overboard while fishing.

While flounder are the primary target for anglers using killies, these baits will also catch just about anything in tidal waters. I have personally used them to catch weakfish, big croaker, striped bass, black sea bass and bluefish, although the latter will often take the tail and leave you the head.

Mummichogs can be caught in minnow traps set in quiet waters and baited with crab or fish, but most anglers buy them from a tackle shop. Even with today's prices it is possible to purchase a day's supply for under $5.00.

Quite often killies are fished along with another bait. Strips of squid are popular as are Gulp! 4-inch swimming mullets. Adding a strip of Mylar, some feathers or spinner blades to the hook is another technique used by flounder fishermen.

Some anglers use a single circle hook on an 18- to 24-inch leader, while others like a two-hook rig with a long leader for the bottom hook and a shorter leader on top. A few folks will use a very long (up to 36-inch) leader with their live minnows. I have trouble detecting a pickup with a leader this long. Once again, the hook is placed up from the bottom jaw and out the top. As with most live baits, the target fish must be given time to get the hook in its mouth. A dropback is necessary, but the timing is subject to much discussion. I drop my rod tip when I feel a bite, then raise it back up until the line comes tight. I know very successful flounder fishermen who dropback for a much longer time. You should use whatever works best for you.

PILCHARDS

The name pilchard is used to cover several types of scaled sardine found in Florida. I have seen what must have been millions of them off the coat of the Keys, where mates using cast nets landed them by the thousands before heading offshore. They may be caught using Sabiki rigs as well.

Once boats are on the fishing grounds, pilchards are used to live-line everything from sailfish to dolphin. Sometimes the boat will anchor or drift over structure, tossing out pilchards like chum. This may attract cobia, king mackerel, barracuda, snapper and even grouper.

My one and only Atlantic sailfish was caught on the way back from a trip to the Hump off of the Keys when the mate saw the sail on the surface, had the captain stop the boat and tossed a live pilchard to the fish. He handed me the rod, I set the hook and had a fantastic fight before releasing the sail.

LIVE TUNAS

Live tuna are used to catch blue and black marlin. The tunas are caught by trolling with handlines, and then the bait is either used immediately or put in a tuna tube until needed. Tuna tubes are PVC plastic pipes that are plumbed—running water from a pump to the bottom of the tube and out the top—to pump water up and over the tuna while it rests nose down in the tube. Large boats may have six or more tuna tubes on the transom.

The tuna are bridled with the rigging line going through the eyes, and then the hook is attached by tying it to the bridle. There are devices designed to make this process much easier and can be purchased from tackle shops specializing in offshore fishing.

The only time I have used tuna for bait was in Panama when fishing for black marlin. The mate caught two tuna on the handline, had them bridled and back in the water in less time than it takes to tell about it. When a marlin ate the tuna, the captain gave it at least 30 seconds to swallow the bait before going full ahead and using the boat to set the hook. The tuna we used in Panama were about 18 inches long and weighted 3 or 4 pounds. In Hawaii and Australia where grander black marlin roam, they fish with yellowfin tuna that can weight up to 30 pounds.

A bait named for Panama and used to catch sailfish is the Panama strip bait. This bait uses the belly from a small tuna that is sewed to the hook so it appears alive in the water. My one and only Pacific sailfish came on a Panama strip bait tied very quickly by my Panamanian mate and placed in the spread from the long rigger. How something so dead could look so alive remains a mystery to me, but it certainly fooled that sailfish.

EELS

Almost every fish in the sea eats eels at some point during their life cycle. Eels are relatively inexpensive to purchase and easy to store and transport. They do well in a live bait bucket, livewell or in a cooler on ice. The latter is the most practical because the ice will chill them down and make them easier to handle.

It is possible to catch your own eels using eel pots. Before doing so you must check local regulations on the use of these devices. In some areas this is considered commercial fishing, and a special license is required.

All containers used to hold eels must be escape-proof. Eels are very good at squeezing through the smallest hole and once loose in a boat or vehicle, the chances are good that at least one will elude recapture. After a few days it is pretty easy to find the body, but getting the smell out of the car or boat is a more serious problem.

Cold weather and live eels produce big striped bass.

Handling eels is not one of the joys of fishing. Eels are covered with a sticky slime that adheres to everything it touches. The use of a rag to hold the eel while placing the hook is highly recommended.

The location of the hook is pretty much up to the angler. I put the hook up through the lower jaw and out through the top. Others go up through the lower jaw and out through one eye. I have seen anglers hook an eel in the tail. I am not sure why they do this, but it is a bad idea. Pulling an eel through the water backwards will result in a dead eel and since eels do not swim backwards, hooking one through the tail does not result in a natural presentation.

Once hooked, eels must always be fished in a manner that prevents them from twisting themselves up with the leader into a slimy ball. When drifting, get the eel in the water as soon as possible after the hook is in place. The motion of the current should keep the eel straight, so long as you do not drop back too fast and allow the line to go slack. When casting an eel, do not put the rod in a holder or hold it stationary in any way. A live eel must be worked like a lure. A steady retrieve is used to keep it moving and to prevent the eel from getting into mischief.

Most eels are fished while alive, but using a dead eel can also be very effective. To make a dead eel swim a special jig head is used. It is molded to swim with a side-to-side action and carries one hook. I use the jig as-is, but some fishermen rig the eel with a tail hook by running a leader with a hook on the end from the anal vent out through the mouth using a rigging needle. That leader is secured to the hook in the jig. The main leader is tied to the eye on the jig.

It is possible to rig an eel without using the jig. A single hook can be inserted behind the head, with the hook's eye just protruding from the mouth. Use a small cable tie to secure the hook in place, and sew the mouth shut around the hook eye with dental floss. The addition of a black barrel swivel to the eye of the hook can be done

A live eel is a great striper bait.

by using an open-eye Siwash hook and securing the swivel by closing the eye with pliers.

Another way to fish an eel is to use the skin on a plug. I have never done this, but I know eel-skin plugs have been responsible for catching some big stripers. I am sure that somewhere somebody still rigs eel-skin plugs, but I have not seen or heard of this practice for many years. The work involved—skinning the eel, pulling the skin over the end of the plug and tying it off—discourages most anglers, including me. The two plugs favored by eel-skin riggers, the Atom and the Creek Chub Pikie, are still in production if you would like to try your hand at rigging them. The idea is to produce a very large swimming eel plug. Once you separate the skin from the eel, the next trick is getting it back on the plug. In most cases the tail hook is removed and the skin goes on over the back of the plug and is tied off just behind the forward hook. Since striped bass are the primary target and they seldom strike the tail of the bait, the tail hook is not replaced.

When I began fishing offshore in 1973, we would not put a spread overboard without at least one rigged eel. Today rigged eels have fallen out of favor, but they still work. During the White Marlin Open out of Ocean City, Maryland in 2008 I was on the *Penta Gone*, a 51-foot Riviera, and in one day we had three of four white marlin come up on an eel. These eels were rigged with circle hooks, because all billfish tournaments require the use of circle hooks in any natural bait.

When preparing a live eel for use offshore or as a rigged eel when striper fishing, put it in a very heavy salt brine. The brine is made from equal amounts of kosher salt and water. This will kill the eel quickly and toughen up his hide. Next, wipe the eel off using a Brillo pad. This gives the skin a warm, bluish glow.

A brined eel is a pretty tough bait, but it will still decompose if it is not kept in a cold place. A surf bag in the back of a beach buggy in August is not a cool place. Please don't ask how I know.

Rigs for Eels

Drift Rig

Drifting live eels is a popular technique for catching striped bass. The rig is about as simple as it gets. A circle hook is tied to a leader and the leader is attached to a three-way swivel or a fish-finder rig. The length of the leader can vary from 3 to 6 feet and the strength will be between 30- and 50-pound-test.

I prefer to use the three-way swivel rig. I find this rig very effective when drifting with the rod in a holder. The striper can pick up the eel and as soon as he turns away he is hooked. No drop back, no setting the hook. Charter boat captains tell me this technique saves their clients many fish.

In some locations drifting an eel is done under a float. The Concrete Ships located near Kiptopeke on Virginia's Eastern Shore is one spot where this technique is successfully employed. Conventional wisdom says that stripers feed on the bottom, but

Live eel float rig. Note sinker to keep the eel below the bobber.

here they take live eels as shallow as 5 feet. On a few rare occasions 30- to 50-pound bass have been seen chasing eels being retrieved across the surface.

There is nothing fancy or complicated about this rig. The eel is suspended from the float at whatever depth the angler chooses. A small sinker is added above the leader to hold the bait at this depth. In my experience, shallow is often better than deep. Most boats drift two or three rigs at different depths and as soon as someone hooks up, the radio is alive with fellow anglers wanting to know how deep the bait was set. This is followed by a flurry of fishermen adjusting their rigs.

In most cases the bass hits with a solid strike and is hooked before the angler can reach the rod. After that, is a matter of bringing the trophy to the boat.

Surf Rig

Casting a live eel in the surf will produce some impressive stripers. The rig is once again very simple. The 12- to 18-inch leader is

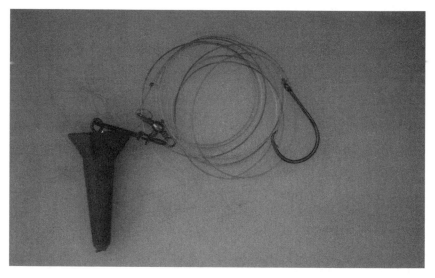

Live bait surf rig.

attached to the running line with a snap swivel. A circle hook is tied to the leader and the eel is cast out into the surf. As soon as it hits the water, the eel must be retrieved at a steady pace to keep it from balling up the leader. Should extra weight be required, a rubber core sinker can be added ahead of the leader.

Moderate to calm surf conditions are best for fishing a live eel. When the water is rough it is difficult for the angler to maintain control of the bait. A rough surf often attracts big stripers so fishing an eel is a good idea, but instead of a live one, rig up a dead eel. It will be tossed around in the surf the same as a live eel, but it won't be able to tangle the leader.

Almost all surf fishing with eels occurs at night. This is the time when big stripers tend to come close to the beach because they feel safer feeding in the shallow water.

MULLET

Like menhaden, mullet are found all along the east coast and are fed upon by most inshore species. They are easier to keep alive than menhaden, and will live for an extended period of time in most types of livewells. It is critical to keep a tight lid on the container, as mullet have a tendency to jump.

Catching a supply of mullet is usually done with a cast net. These fish move down the northeast coast in the fall and tend to stay close to shore, where they can be caught with relative ease. It is also possible to catch a supply of mullet using a haul seine when the bait is in shallow water close to shore. The bays behind the barrier island are prime area for haul seining. I have pulled a small haul net in the ocean for mullet and while that was a memorable occasion, it is not something I would recommend.

Most tackle shops sell fresh mullet, but few keep live ones in stock. If you want to fish with live mullet you will need your own method to keep them in that condition.

Mullet will also be found swimming close to the surface in the back bays and tidal creeks. Once again, a cast net is the best way to catch them.

Most live mullet in the northeast are fished for summer flounder. The mullet is hooked through the lips and fished on a three-way swivel rig. Free-swimming mullet are used as bait for red drum, speckled trout and striped bass.

In the southeast, tarpon are the target of live mullet anglers. The mullet are caught in cast nets and stored in the live well on the boat. Live mullet may also be purchased from bait dealers who supply the guides fishing out of various marinas.

Once the mullet are secured, the angler or guide will anchor up in a location he or she thinks will be productive, and two lines baited with live mullet are put out behind the boat. When a tarpon comes near the mullet he causes the bait to become a bit nervous. This is the signal for the angler to get ready; but when the attack comes, no one is ever really ready.

The tarpon usually jumps as soon as he feels the hook, and in most cases he is successful in separating himself from the annoying piece of metal. In an effort to prevent early separation, the angler should bow to the fish. After the initial jumps the tarpon will settle into a tug-of-war with the angler, which can last quite a while. Once the fish sees the boat he may jump again or keep on pulling. Finally, the fish will give up and allow the mate or guide to pull him to the boat for a quick release. The tarpon should always be resuscitated by running the boat slow ahead until he has regained his strength.

You may hear some anglers complain that bait fishing for tarpon is not as exciting as catching them on a fly or plug. To those people I say, "poppycock!" If there is anything more exciting than watching a big tarpon attack a live mullet I have not yet had that experience. Once the hook is in, the fight is the same on bait, plug or fly.

Rigs for Mullet

Tarpon Rig

The rig used to catch tarpon on a live mullet is nothing more than a hook on a leader. The 6-foot leader is heavy, up to 100-pound-test, because the tarpon can wear through anything less during a long fight. Some anglers use circle hooks, while others continue to use J hooks. An Albright knot is used to attach the leader to the running line.

The same rig is used when fishing a dead mullet bait on the bottom. This is sometimes employed in conjunction with two live baits on the surface to intercept a tarpon that is cruising deep.

Tarpon fishermen from Virginia to Georgia fish dead baits on the bottom as much, if not more, than live baits. The water behind the barrier islands, where most of this tarpon fishing takes place, is shallow, so the bait may be held on the bottom with a relatively light weight. If the fish are in or near an inlet where the water is deeper

A live mullet ready for his date with a tarpon.

Tarpon caught on a live mullet.

and the current is stronger, a heavier weight will be required. Adding a sinker to a tarpon rig gives the fish another bit of leverage to make it easier for him to come unglued. Believe me, a tarpon does not need any more help, but if it takes a sinker to put the bait in the strike zone, than a sinker must be used.

SPOT AND PINFISH

These small fish are used for snook, flounder, striped bass, speckled trout, weakfish and tarpon, to name just a few species. They are not that difficult to catch on tiny pieces of bait or a Sabiki rig. Both will stay alive in an aerated tank without the need for outside plumbing.

In recent years, with the size limit on summer flounder increasing to more than 20 inches in some states, live spot have become the go-to bait for those trying to catch a flounder large enough to keep.

Spot are used in the Maryland portion of the Chesapeake Bay during the summer to catch striped bass. A live spot placed in one of the many well-known locations throughout the bay just about guarantees a striper on the end of the line. I am constantly amazed that even during summer weekends, the striper fishing with live spot holds up under those crowded conditions.

I have almost as much fun catching the bait as I do catching the stripers. Using light tackle and a top-bottom rig baited with blood-worms, we often have spot on two at a time. At times the large spot outnumber the small ones and we have to move the boat looking for bait-size fish. This is one of the few situations where fishermen complain about catching fish that are too big. Since I love spot as a primary ingredient for a fish fry, the larger ones find their way into the fish box, while the smaller ones go into the livewell.

In more tropical areas, pinfish are used to tempt snook, grouper and speckled trout. They also attract jacks, barracuda and sharks and these fish can put some real excitement in your day.

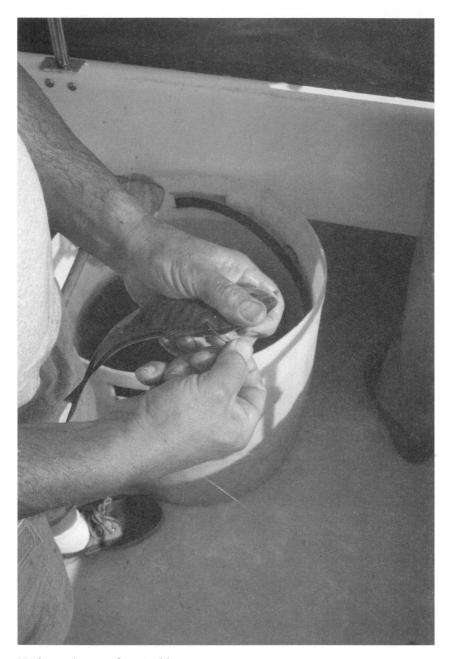

Hooking a live spot for striped bass.

Pinfish are caught much the same way as spot and stored in a livewell. When fishing for snook or grouper the bait is tossed under overhanging mangrove branches. Allowed to swim without any weight, the pinfish moves just outside the mangrove roots and the fish attack from unseen locations. The angler must use as much force as necessary to get his fish out from the tangle of roots and into open water, sometimes before he is sure what type of fish he has hooked. This mystery only adds to the excitement.

Pinfish used for speckled trout are fished in the deep holes where the largest of the species live. This technique will work all year, but is especially productive during the winter. I have taken pinfish and spot offshore and fed them to amberjack, who are really not very selective in their diet. They also work on crevalle jacks and just about any fish that eats other fish.

Rigs for Spot and Pinfish

Summer Flounder Rig

Summer flounder lie on the bottom waiting for a meal to pass by, so the prudent angler will make sure the bait he is using swims past the hidden flatfish. Flounder feed in very shallow as well as deep water, and the rigs used to fish the various depths will vary.

When fishing water less than ten feet deep I do not use any weight. The spot will find the bottom quickly and stay there as the boat drifts along. This is the basic free-swimming rig described earlier. Should conditions conspire to move the boat at a speed where the bait comes off the bottom, add a rubber core sinker ahead of the leader.

In deeper water, a three-way swivel rig will allow the addition of a sinker that is heavy enough to keep the spot in the strike zone. I do use a longer leader, 2 to 3 feet, because this gives the bait more freedom of movement.

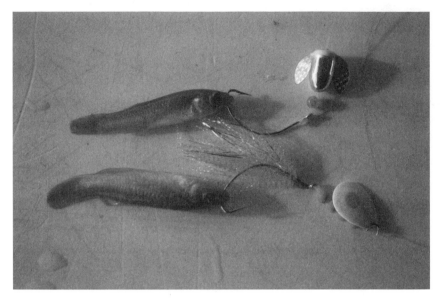

Live minnows on flounder rigs.

Many flounder fishermen employ a fish-finder rig to allow the flounder to take the bait without feeling the weight of the sinker. I find the three-way swivel rig, when used with a circle hook, is equally effective when the angler gives a short dropback before allowing the line to come tight.

Float Rig
Live bait fishing from shore, bridges, piers or from an anchored boat requires a different presentation than fishing from a moving boat. The bait must move along the bottom while the angler remains stationary.

In order to accomplish this trick a float is used. The rig is set at a depth below the float that corresponds to the depth of the water. The depth of the deepest area to be covered should be used. If the water becomes shallow over a bar or shoal the bait will be a ways behind the float, which is better than having the bait off the bottom.

A single live bait can be fished under the float by simply using a snap-swivel to connect a hook and leader. This would work well with live spot or pinfish.

The terminal rig used under a float when fishing with minnows goes back to the old days of flounder fishing. A spreader rig that keeps both hooks on the bottom is ideal in this situation. The hooks are attached to the outside of the spreader bar and the sinker goes in the middle.

The float will move along in the current or under the influence of the wind. Generally the wind has greater influence when fishing from a pier or bridge because there is more line above the water. When fishing from an anchored boat the float will go off in the current and the boat must be positioned so the rig will cover the most productive bottom.

Float rigs are used from piers to fish a live bait for king mackerel, cobia and tarpon. In this situation a second line is cast out and acts as a trolley rig. This line is anchored to the bottom with a heavy sinker and the live bait float rig is connected to it with a release clip. When a fish hits, the line is released and the fight is on.

Most of the live bait used on piers is caught on site by the angler. He or she will first cast out the trolley line and then catch a bluefish. As soon as the blue hits the deck, he is hooked to the main line and sent down to the water. With the main line baited up, the angler will return to his lighter outfit and try to build a supply of bait. Baits are kept in a bucket or basket tied to the pier and lowered into the water until they are needed.

LIVE SHRIMP

Live shrimp are used to catch red drum, tarpon, bonefish, pompano, speckled trout, weakfish, snappers, whiting, and many others. Several species of shrimp find their way onto hooks, from the South-Atlantic all the way around to the Gulf of Mexico.

A bait shrimp.

I have never seen live shrimp, other than grass shrimp, sold in a tackle shop north of North Carolina and very few places have them there. Moving further south it becomes more common to find live shrimp, and in Florida just about every shop has a good supply.

I have captured shrimp in a haul net while fishing in North Carolina, but I was with a man who had a commercial license. Different states have different laws about netting shrimp, so checking current regulations would be advised.

There is one species of shrimp that should come with a warning. The manta shrimp has the ability to split a thumbnail using the hard protrusion on its shell. While not widely used as bait, it is on the diet of flounder, striped bass and big trout. I have never seen them sold in tackle shops, but it is possible to catch manta shrimp over muddy bottoms using small hooks and baits.

In the Florida Keys, live shrimp are the primary bait for just about everything that swims. In most situations the shrimp is impaled on a hook and cast to fish seen in shallow water. Allowed to move on the bottom without any weight, the presentation is very natural and the technique effective. The key to success is accurate casting and a gentle entry by the shrimp. The bait is cast in front of the fish with the hope that he will find it as he feeds along the bottom. Casting behind or over the fish may not result in success. Casting right on top of a bonefish or red drum will usually clear the area very quickly. I have seen some impressive tarpon caught on a little live shrimp and my largest bonefish, estimated by the guide to weigh between 8 and 9 pounds, came on a live shrimp.

Most anglers hook a live shrimp through the hard shell near the head. They will also hook them through the tail. Both hooking positions seem to work about the same. The hook is usually a light wire model so as not to damage the bait.

Live wells will keep shrimp alive for a long time. They also stay healthy in minnow buckets that are lowered into the water from a boat, pier, or bridge.

Shrimp hooked in the tail with a circle hook.

Grass shrimp are very small and almost transparent. They are a mainstay on the diet of numerous fish from white perch to weakfish. Generally fished on small hooks and often under a bobber, they are very popular during the spring perch run in eastern tidal rivers and creeks. Hook two or three shrimp at the same time and let them drift through a spillway or in a tidal rip.

In shallow bays, chumming with grass shrimp is a common practice. Weakfish and striped bass are just two species that will gather for a shrimp feast. Since this is done in shallow water, stealth is required. The boat is anchored near a dropoff or at the mouth of a feeder creek. Grass shrimp are deployed into the current with hopes that the larger fish will follow the food to the boat. Early morning, late evening or nighttime are best for this technique. Anglers may bait up with grass shrimp, or cast small jigs tipped with shrimp into the chum line. Some very impressive weakfish have been caught using this method.

Rigs for Shrimp

Live Shrimp Rig
A live shrimp rig is tied using a light leader or line and a wire hook. I have not used a circle hook with live shrimp, mainly because I don't get to the Keys very often, but I believe they would work just fine.

The shrimp is cast out on light spinning tackle, either to fish spotted in shallow water or under mangroves or other structure. A live shrimp appeals to a gamefish because it is a primary staple of the fish's natural diet, and when fished on light tackle the shrimp makes a natural presentation.

When fishing the shallow water of the Keys the angler almost always sees the target fish take the shrimp. The trick is not to strike too soon or too late. Too soon, and the angler will pull the bait out of the fish's mouth. Too late, and all you get back is an empty hook.

I once fed several shrimp to a pair of sheepshead who were grateful for the free meal. I could see then take the shrimp, but I was unable to put the hook in their thieving little mouths.

Popping Cork Rig

A quiet presentation is required when casting live shrimp in shallow water, but the popping cork is just the opposite. Here the cork makes a commotion on the surface while the shrimp rides along behind. This technique is very effective over grass beds and when fishing muds. (Muds are areas of disturbed water where speckled trout or redfish are feeding.) I have caught trout on every cast fishing muds north of Key Largo.

Speckled trout are the primary target for this technique, but it works on red drum as well. The ever-present jacks find the added nose of the popping cork too good to resist.

The same rig as used when sight casting, a single wire hook tied to the end of the running line is used here with the cork set 12 to 24 inches above the hook. The rig is cast out and retrieved using a twitching motion of the rod tip. This action makes the cork splash and the shrimp jerk. A brief pause every few seconds is recommended to give the shrimp a chance to slowly sink. This is when many strikes occur.

It is very exciting when a big trout or drum pulls the cork under, and setting the hook requires an immediate response. There will be some slack line on the water between the cork and the rod, and this must be taken out by cranking the reel while lifting the rod tip. Once the line comes tight the hook can be set.

Shrimp on a Jig

Shrimp on a jig is not a new recipe by Bobby Flay. It is a way to present a shrimp when conditions require a bit more weight. As previously mentioned, I have caught pompano, jacks, speckled trout, Spanish mackerel and even a small cobia using this method.

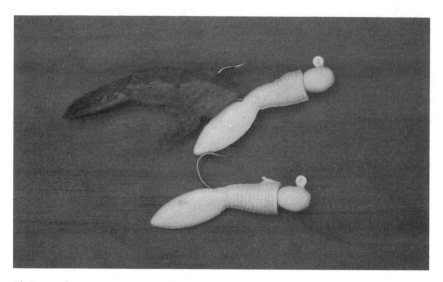

Shrimp tail on a pompano jig.

A jig is usually employed in deeper water where a live, unweighted shrimp would not be able to reach fish lurking on or near the bottom. The jig may also be required if the wind makes casting a shrimp all but impossible.

There are leadheads made for this style of fishing and sold as pompano jigs. The ones I have came with a small yellow paddle tail. Plain jigs with no added attractors are also used. The shrimp is hooked through the tail, and they remain alive for an extended period of time.

From a boat or shore the jig and shrimp combo is cast out and allowed to swing by in the current. When fishing from a bridge or pier, the leadhead and shrimp may be cast and retrieved or jigged vertically close to the structure.

Worms

Bloodworms and sandworms are the two most popular of these crawly creatures. While very effective when fishing for spot, croaker, trout, white perch and other small fishes, some very large striped bass have been landed on worms.

Bloodworms are dug from the mud at low tide by some hard-working men and women. A TV show that highlighted dirty jobs did an episode on worm digging and from what I saw this is not an easy career choice. New England and Canada provide most of the worms for the rest of the coast.

In order to assure that the worms arrive alive, they are shipped via air, which is one reason why they are expensive. Another reason for the high cost of worms is the fact that no one has figured out how to raise them commercially. Every worm must be dug by hand during low tide, which only occurs once or perhaps twice during daylight hours.

Bloodworms are used from Maine to North Carolina, while sandworms are seldom sold south of New Jersey. I have been told that the shelf life of a sandworm is much shorter than a bloodworm. I know when I managed a tackle shop the bloodworms I received on Thursday were pretty well shot by Sunday night. It is a happy shop owner who sees the last of his bloodworms go out the door on Sunday afternoon.

Anglers should inspect the package of bloodworms before purchase. The animals must be more pink than red, and any sign of blood in the bottom of the bag signals a product that is not fresh.

Bloodworms are packed in seaweed and should be kept cool and dry. While many tackle shops sell bloodworms in bags with mixed sizes, others go to the trouble of sorting them out by size. When it is possible to purchase all large bloodworms, do so—even though the smaller worms are less expensive. Big bloodworms provide more baits per worm when fishing pieces for spot or kingfish. Using a large bloodworm streaming out behind the hook when striper fishing provides much more movement than a shorter specimen. They are tougher than small worms and seem to last longer on the hook.

Freshwater will turn your worms into an expensive mess. Freezer packs are better than ice for keeping bloodworms in prime condition. When purchased the day before the trip, I keep my bloodworms in the refrigerator overnight. In the morning I put the bait in a small cooler along with one or two freezer packs to keep the worms dry and cool. I have tried salting and freezing leftover worms and the results were not very successful. Now I either toss them away or add them to my chum bag in the freezer.

When using worms for small fish a Chestertown hook is a good choice. The worm is cut into small pieces and then slid over the hook. Once a bloodworm is cut, he does not retain his flavor for very long. The prudent angler will change his bait every 10 minutes or so. I keep my cutting board with pieces of bloodworm in the cooler, as this bait will quickly dry out.

Bloodworms do have a small set of pinchers in their heads. It is possible for one to pinch a hand or finger, but to the best of my knowledge, the bite is seldom fatal. Head-boat mates delight in hanging a bloodworm from their hand and entertaining the children and some of the adults on board.

Striped bass will take a bloodworm or a sandworm with most of this fishing done from the beach during the spring run. When fished in the surf, two worms are placed on one hook. The first worm is balled up, while the second is allowed to stream out in the current. This early season fishing will try the patience of any angler as bites are few and far between. However, when a striper does pick up the bait, she is often the trophy of a lifetime.

While most worm fishing for stripers is done on a cold and windy spring beach, there have been occasions during warm weather when a wayward striper picked up a worm meant for a lesser fish. More than one summer surf fisherman has been surprised when a big bass took a liking to that small piece of bloodworm fished for spot, whiting or croaker.

I have seen instances when weakfish wanted a bloodworm and nothing else. This is usually a spring event, as these fish lose their taste for worms as the summer wears on.

Winter flounder are another species that loves a bloodworm. Here too the best fishing is in the spring when the little flatfish are in the back bays. I have personally caught a few good sized summer flounder on bloodworms. This was another accidental catch on bait set for winter flounder, spot or whiting.

Rigs for Worms

Surf Rig
Fishing worms in the surf is normally done with the basic two-hook top-bottom rig. Small fish require the use of a long shanked Chestertown hook, while larger fish such as striped bass call for a circle hook.

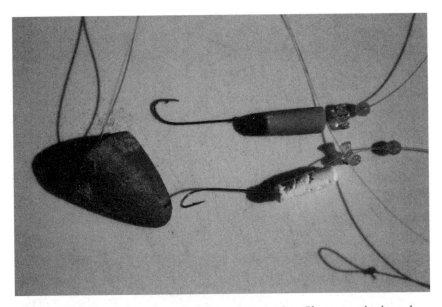

Surf rig for kingfish (sea mullet, roundheads, whiting). Note Chestertown hooks and small floats with beads.

Spot and croaker fishermen like to add a few beads and blades, while striper fishermen normally go with an unadorned hook. The rig used for springtime stripers is a three-way swivel setup. Since the wait for a bite is usually long, the rod is set in a sand spike. The circle hook lends itself well to this still fishing, and the striper is often hooked before the angler can reach the rod.

Trolling Rig

There are two basic trolling rigs used with worms. The first is a Colorado spinner blade placed ahead of a hook baited with a large blood or sandworm. The rig is slow-trolled in shallow water over grass or rocks where stripers are found. The technique is very effective when employed from a row boat, canoe or kayak. These boats create very little noise that could spook fish in this skinny water.

The second trolling rig consists of a tube lure trailing a large blood or sandworm. Used primarily in New England around areas

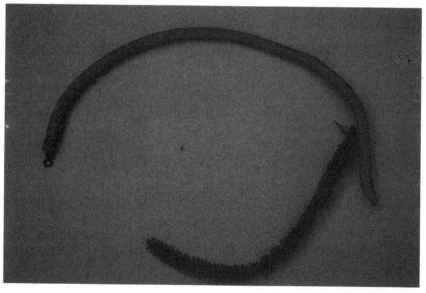

A worm and tube rig. (Gulp! worm used for demonstration).

where large rocks form reefs, such as the infamous Sow and Pigs off of Cuttyhunk, this rig has produced some of the largest striped bass ever caught. Once again a very slow presentation is required, but these dangerous waters are no place for small boats or inexperienced operators.

Due to the strong current and deep water, wire line is used to put the tube and worm rig in the strike zone. Attention must be paid to water depth, with line let out and taken in as the bottom contour changes.

CLAMS

Used everywhere from deep water for cod to the surf for striped bass, clams are a very versatile bait. They come prepackaged in a hard case and will keep for several days on ice. When ready for use, two clams are smashed together with one usually cracking open. At this point the broken clam is scooped out of the shell and prepared

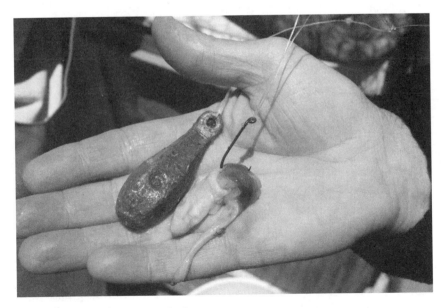

A clam bait ready for a trip to the bottom.

for the hook, while the survivor is used to break open the next victim.

In most cases quahogs (large clams, up to three inches in diameter) are the clams used for bait. Smaller clams will work, but are much more expensive than their larger cousins. Quahogs are caught by commercial boats fishing in the ocean. The larger boats usually fish for the seafood market, where big clams wind up as clam strips served in restaurants. Smaller clam boats fish close to shore primarily for the bait trade.

One technique employed in the spring for striped bass involves anchoring down-current from a working clam boat and fishing clams on the bottom. The boat provides a natural chum line that draws stripers to the bait. Cooperation between the clam boat and the fishing boat is necessary to make this system work. Too often, unknowing or uncaring recreational fishing boats will impede the work of the clam boat and become a danger to themselves and the commercial boat. If you keep a safe distance and behave yourself the clam boat can help you catch fish.

When purchasing clams for bait they should be closed and have a reasonably clean smell. Broken or open clams are not much good unless you subscribe to the strangely New Jersey notion that "rotters" make a great bait for stripers. I have known surf fishermen from the Garden State who seek out the oldest, deadest clams from the bottom of the bag or cooler to use for bait. They claim these baits are close in texture and smell to a clam that has broken and washed ashore after a storm. While their logic may be correct, the result is a bait that leaves a reminder in the cooler or vehicle used to transport it to the beach.

Two years ago a rotter escaped from the possession of a Jersey angler whom I had invited to fish in Delaware. I did not use my truck for a few days after the trip, and when I opened the door the stench just about knocked me over. I found the offending clam and removed it, but I do believe his perfume still lingers in my truck.

Drum, both black and red, enjoy a clam meal. Whole clams fished on the bottom account for more of these big fish than any other bait.

The usual manner of fishing for drum with clams involves anchoring the boat in a likely drum hangout and dropping a clam to the bottom. The broken shells from the opening procedure are dropped to the bottom and act as chum. Some anglers allow the shells to flutter down and disperse on their own, while others put the shells in an onion bag and drop them down with a heavy weight to hold the chum in place. A few of the more athletic among us use a baseball bat to launch clam pieces to the far flung regions around the boat. At one point in my fishing career, I decided if hitting a clam shell with a baseball bat was good, hitting whole clams would be better. My hands still sting just remembering the meeting of clam and aluminum bat.

When fishing for drum around hard structure, put the clam on a bucktail or other leadhead and jig over or cast to the fish. Bottom fishing in this situation will result in more lost rigs than fish caught, while controlling the bait on the jig keeps it working in the strike zone.

In this situation it may be a good idea to drop some busted-up clams in one location, and then go away for an hour or less. When you return the chum should have the drum concentrated in that location. The risk you take is another angler discovering your secret spot before you return.

Tog, triggerfish, porgies and black sea bass are just a few of the bottom feeders that enjoy a clam meal. It does take a deft touch on the rod to set the hook before these superb bait stealers get a free meal. The use of braided line has moved the odds of a successful hookup in the angler's favor.

When Claude Bain, then Director of the Virginia Saltwater Fishing Tournament, and a few close friends were trying to find a bait to catch the spadefish that had become abundant in Virginia

Tog may be caught on crab, clam or bloodworm.

waters, it was the lowly clam that won the day. We knew spadefish liked jellyfish, but attempts to get a jellyfish on a hook were less than successful. Further study revealed that spades also ate mussels, but once again, that bait proved difficult to use. Finally, we tried small pieces of clam and had remarkably good success.

Spadefish are easy to find, as they cruise around or over hard structure. Getting them to eat can be a problem. The accepted method is to anchor up-current from the structure and to chum with the soft belly of the clam. The foot is cut into tiny pieces and placed on a small circle hook. The baited hook is allowed to move towards the structure, either unweighted or with a split shot or two. To better control the depth of the bait, the hook can be suspended at various lengths below a bobber.

Now comes the important part. Place the rod in a holder and do not pick it up until it bends over under the strain of a fish. If you hold the rod and try to set the hook yourself, you will miss the spadefish. I do not know why, but spades will tap-tap-tap the bait many times before finally taking. It is a well-controlled angler who can stand there through all those bites without trying to hook the fish.

As mentioned previously, spades can be very frustrating. There can be hundreds of them swimming around the boat, and not one will take the bait. When this occurs the best thing to do is pack up and go looking for more cooperative fish. I have had days when we moved three or four times before finding spadefish willing to eat.

Rigs for Clams

Surf Rig

When fishing with clam in the surf I use a short leader on a three-way swivel rig. A circle hook on 8 to 12 inches of 50-pound Fluorocarbon leader is all that is required. The short leader makes it easier to cast and the Fluorocarbon is tough, invisible and stiffer than fishing line. Do not put any float, spinners or feathers on this rig.

Casting a soft clam any distance into the surf can be difficult. A gentle lob cast will do the job when distance is not a problem, but any attempt to throw 100 yards into an onshore wind can separate the clam from the hook. To compensate for this problem, try tying the bait on the hook with dental floss. Another way to keep hook and clam together is to put the bait in a small mesh bag made from a used pair of pantyhose. The bag is then tied to the hook.

Clams are a particularly good bait in the Atlantic surf after a hard northeast blow. The large waves generated by the strong onshore wind will dig up and break open clams, making for an easy meal not only for striped bass, but all bottom-feeding fish. At times it is possible to find all the bait you need by walking the shoreline at low tide.

Clam is seldom used to catch small fish in the surf, because it is soft and can easily be removed from the hook. I have used it to catch kings, spot, and croaker from the beach when the water was relatively calm and the bite was hot. The use of circle hooks helps to catch those bait stealers on this soft bait. Clam is also a very good choice when small black drum invade the surf.

Cod Rig

Cod will gladly take a clam in both shallow and deep water. Sometimes a cod fisherman will combine a clam and a Diamond jig or tube lure on his rig. The clam has the scent, and the jig or tube the action to attract the cod. Also, if the clam is taken without a hookup, the jig or tube will be there when the next cod swims past.

MUSSELS

Another shellfish that can be used for bait is the mussel. It is unusual to find mussels for sale in a tackle shop, so in most cases it will be necessary to catch your own. They are easily found at low tide clinging to rocks and pilings, where they may be scraped off using heavy-duty gloves, trowels or a paint scraper.

Scraping off mussels results in many of them being broken open, and these must be used right away. The rest can be put on ice, where they will last for a day or two.

Like clams, mussels are a soft bait that fish can easily remove from the hook. In spite of this, they make an excellent offering for tog, sheepshead and triggerfish.

Mussels, with their brittle shells and soft meat, make great chum. I put them in a bag and crush them with a hammer or similar device. This crushed-up mess is placed in a chum bucket and lowered to the bottom. Since just about every fish that feeds over hard structure eats mussels, this chum will have them coming from far and wide.

CRABS

"The bait that bites back," crabs come in all shapes and sizes. Blue claw, green, mole, speckled, hermit and fiddler crabs all produce excellent results. There may be other crabs used in locations throughout the country, but I suspect their use is similar to the way we fish with crabs on the east coast.

BLUE CLAW

The blue claw crab is found from New England to Texas, and is used for bait throughout its range. In the mid-Atlantic, where blue claws are an important commercial and recreational species, the laws governing their capture and possession are varied and strongly enforced. Crabs purchased from a tackle shop will conform to local laws because the business owner does not want to risk his license, but when you set out to catch your own bait, it is a good idea to read and reread the law.

In most fishing situations, blue claw crabs are cut into sections and fished on a top-bottom rig. They are an excellent bait for a variety of species, including tog, sea bass, sheepshead and croaker.

I often carry blue claws when fishing the long range head boats out of North Carolina. While these boats don't go out for days at a time like the ones in California, they do run well off in the Atlantic on 12-, 18- and 24-hour trips. Frozen cigar minnows and squid are usually provided by the boat, but fresh bait is not. I find the cut-up blue claws draw attention from grouper, grunts, African pompano, vermillion snappers, and triggerfish. The crabs are easy to transport in the same cooler you will use to carry your catch home.

In the winter, when fresh bait is at a premium along the northeast coast, live crabs are available from dredgers who work the Chesapeake and Delaware bays. This practice has come under criticism from conservation groups who feel that the crabs, who are mostly females with eggs, should be left in the mud to replenish the stock in the spring. While I do agree with this position, I will continue to use those crabs for tog bait until the government shuts the dredgers down.

In the Florida Keys small crabs are drifted alive for tarpon and permit. The crabs are hooked in the shell close to the back fin and allowed to swim in the current. I have seen tarpon caught on this bait, and was surprised that a fish that big would inhale a crab that small.

PEELERS

A peeler crab, also known as a shedder in some locations, is one who is about to molt or shed its hard shell. Females can only breed during this process, and the males, or jimmies, will cradle the females under their body until breeding is complete. These are known as doublers.

Peelers are also coveted by commercial crabbers, who will hold them in tanks until the shed is complete and then harvest the resulting soft-shell crab. Due to their value, peelers can command a high price. During times when peelers are in short supply they can fetch several dollars each, but when the market is flooded the price drops considerably.

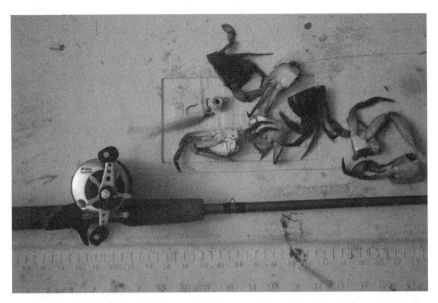

Cut peeler crab fished on a Tsunami ball jig.

When a female is about to molt, she releases a scent that attracts a male. The problem with this system is that every creature in the sea is aware that this scent means easy pickin's for a crab dinner. I believe this is why peelers make much better baits than hard crabs. I also believe this scent is lost if the crab dies and is frozen.

I know of fishermen who use soft crabs for bait. I will never do this because there is nothing that comes out of the water I would rather eat than a soft crab, and I am not going to feed my dinner to a fish.

Back in the 1960s and early 70s, Chesapeake Bay anglers would float soft crabs into shallow water over grass beds and catch some impressive stripers. This was done on still, warm summer nights. Today, the stripers are back, but grass beds are not and this technique is seldom used.

The great weakfish run in the 1970s and 80s was a good time for peeler crabs. While popular in the Delaware Bay, they were a staple for fishermen working the Tangier Sound out of Crisfield, Maryland. The sound drops off from 15 to over 100 feet along its eastern edge, and every evening you would find charter and private boats lined up along this ridge. The weakfish or trout would move up from the deep water on their way to the grass beds close to shore, with but one thing on their mind: soft crabs. Anglers would drop peeler-baited hooks to the bottom where the trout could easily find them. The fish would pass by in small groups, and you could mark their progress by the shouts of "Fish on!" or "Get the net!" emanating from different boats.

Almost from the beginning of the trout run, jigs were the most popular enticer for Delaware Bay anglers. Quite often those jigs were tipped with peeler crab which greatly improves their success.

Sometime in the 1990s, in a misguided attempt to save money, someone used chicken breast soaked in peeler oil and caught a trout. This practice is still employed, even though several fishermen

Peeler crab on a top-bottom rig.

have contracted salmonella from handling the chicken and then their lunch.

To prepare a peeler for bait, first remove the apron and then the hard outer shell by putting the thumb underneath the back and prying upward. Toss the hard shell away and cut the body into sections. If using the claws as separate baits, crack the outer shell and put the hook through the knuckle. I find gentle pressure with my fishing pliers is enough to crack the shell of the claw.

Peeler is another soft bait that will quickly fall off the hook if not properly impaled. The crab is cut into sections, and each section has holes where the legs were. Put the hook through one of these holes and the bait will stay in place. A hook that penetrates the shell will soon work a large hole and fall out. As with clams, it is possible to tie the bait on with dental floss or a rubber band.

The size of the bait depends on the size of the target fish. While a small piece of peeler will attract weakfish, puppy drum, and stripers, it takes a larger section to bring in a big red or black drum.

When fishing for trout, I will cut a peeler body into four sections and, with the claws and apron, this produces seven baits from one crab. I will cut the body in half when fishing for big reds, leaving the legs and the claws intact. The joint where the back fin attaches to the shell is ideal for placing the hook when using a half-crab bait.

Rigs for Peeler Crabs

Peeler Crab Rig
A top-bottom rig is the most common rig used when fishing with peeler crab. The addition of feathers, blades and other adornments is also common.

A single hook three-way swivel rig is used in the surf when drum are the target. Fish-finder rigs are also employed in this fishery, but I find the three-way swivel rig easier to cast.

As with almost all bait rigs, the use of circle hooks is highly recommended.

GREEN CRABS

These nasty smelling little gems have become the go-to bait for tog fishermen. While native to the northern states, green crabs are now found in tackle shops as far south as Virginia.

Green crabs are not as big as blue claws and are usually cut into halves. Especially large specimens may be quartered. The hook is placed through a leg hole as it is in blue claws.

Green crabs are a hardy species. They can be kept in a minnow trap and will live a long time with the occasional feeding.

The late Russ Wilson kept his two minnow traps full of green crabs tied off the transom of his boat. Each trap received one or two whole mackerel each week and those crabs were as happy as clams.

This mate is cutting green crabs for tog.

Less happy were the guests Russ invited to fish from his boat. Just before casting off from the dock, Russ would flip those minnow traps full of green crabs and rotten mackerel into the motor well. As the boat slowly moved down the river, the stench would waft up from the stern and overcome anyone with even a slightly weak stomach. Some of his guests would think there must be a week-old dead body in the water next to the boat, while others were too busy at the rail to think or care about where the odor originated from.

Once the boat was running on plane the odor was held at bay. On the fishing grounds, Russ would deftly cut the crabs into fishable sections and leave them on the bait board for all to use. By this time one was either used to the smell or very unhappy. Unhappy people who complained to the captain received very little consolation.

Rigs for Green Crabs

Tog Rig

A tog rig should be made using as little material as possible. I use a section of 50-pound fishing line with a perfection loop in one end, a double surgeon's loop in the other, and a dropper loop in between. No snaps, no swivels, no hardware at all. I do use a snap to connect the rig to my running line. A six to ten foot section of 50-pound line is attached to the braided line from my reel with an Albright knot. The snap is tied to this shock leader with an improved clinch knot.

Tog live in some very rough neighborhoods and the loss of tackle is an accepted part of the fishing. Since there is no doubt that you are going to lose rigs, why donate any more tackle to the bottom than absolutely necessary? It is wise to check the rig and the shock leader for wear before every drop. While most rigs are lost to snags, some are lost to wear and those usually have a nice tog on the end.

I find one-hook rigs are better that two-hook rigs when tog fishing. Having a second hook dangling about is an open invitation to the local snags. It is going to cost you enough one-hook rigs during a day of fishing; using a two-hook rig will only increase the loss. I also believe that a two-hook rig can cost you a fish. Tog do all they can to get back inside the structure and cut your line. They already take the sinker with them and it often hangs up, but the surgeon's loop is weak and should break. The hook is held in place with a dropper loop that is also a weak knot, but why take the chance that it just might hold long enough for the tog to get away?

Tog is one species where I can say that a circle hook is no more effective than a J hook. If you have a chance to visit an aquarium where tog are kept, go during feeding time and watch the way a tog eats. They suck the food to their teeth, crush it and spit out the shell. The hook does not get inside their mouths, let alone down their gullets, so the circle hook cannot do its job. Braided line and quick reflexes are the key to successful tog fishing. Many tog experts swear by Virginia-style hooks. I have had good luck using these, as well as wide-gap live-bait hooks. In either case make sure that the hook is strong, and can take the pressure of a big tog pulling down with all his might.

HERMIT AND FIDDLER CRABS

Hermit and fiddler crabs are used to catch tog as well as sheepshead. The fiddler crab is more likely to be sold in tackle shops and is a bit easier to use. Fiddlers live in the mud alongside tidal creeks and are frequently found in large colonies. Chasing them around in the mud will work to catch them and will provide entertainment for anyone watching, but using a bit of ingenuity is better.

Find a location where fiddler crabs are plentiful and dig a few holes large enough to hold a coffee can. Bury the can so the lip is even with the surface and wait for the crabs to fall in. When enough fiddlers are captured, dig up the cans and go fishing.

Most anglers hook a fiddler crab through the body on the opposite side from the one large claw. They tend to stay on the hook quite well and will catch fish when nothing else seems to work.

I once fished for tog and sheepshead with two very experienced anglers who assured me that peeler crab would work as well as a fiddler crab. The boat anchored next to us did have fiddlers, while we did not. That boat also had a good catch of tog and sheepshead, while we did not.

I have never tried to capture hermit crabs, but have found plenty by accident. These are the same animals sold in pet shops along with a cage, food and decorations. Those used as bait do not come with glow-in-the-dark paint and silver glitter.

To fish with a hermit crab it must first be removed from its shell. A gentle but firm strike with a hammer usually does the trick. Strike too hard and you get crab dip; too soft and the shell remains intact.

Hermit crabs are fished much the same way as fiddler crab. The hook is placed in the body, which is much softer than the shell on any other crab. I know they make a good bait, but in my opinion they are too soft to stay on the hook and a pain to open. I will stick with the fiddlers.

MOLE CRABS

Mole crabs, or sand fleas, live in the surf zone where they may be caught by hand or using rakes made for this task. The trick is to dig quickly as the waves recede and to catch all you can before the next wave comes ashore. If you have small children it is usually easy to bribe them to catch the crabs while you snooze under the sun.

In areas where mole crabs are used it is possible to purchase all you need for a reasonable price. Even during the dead of winter, frozen crabs are available and used successfully on tog. These are the only crab baits that work almost as well frozen as they do alive.

Special rake used to catch mole crabs (sand fleas) in the surf.

Once captured or purchased, the crabs must be kept in slightly damp—but never wet—sand. They do not have to be covered with sand, just enough to keep them happy. If you put mole crabs in a container full of sand and water they will die.

Mole crabs do go through the molting process and soft crabs seem to be better baits. I also like to use female crabs with eggs.

Hook at least two crabs at a time on one hook as they are easily removed by fish. Put the hook in the belly and out the hard shell on the top. This shell will crack, and sooner or later the hole will open up large enough for the crab to come off. Always check the condition of the bait every few minutes to be sure there is still something on the hook.

In the surf, mole crabs are prime baits for whiting. It is possible to keep a fresh supply on the hook just by digging up a few as you fish.

One of my favorite uses for mole crabs is drifting them around rocks in pursuit of striped bass. I place two crabs on a single circle

Live mole crab on a surf rig.

hook and let them float around close to and even in the rocks. During periods of strong current I may place a split shot or two ahead of the leader, but in most cases I fish the sand fleas unweighted.

Drifting mole crabs is generally more productive after dark, but I have seen late fall days when the stripers could not leave them alone. On one such afternoon I was catching stripers at a good clip and passing them to my wife's aunt, who cleaned and cooked the fish in her camper before putting one or two on a plate and passing them back to me while I was still fishing. They were the freshest fish I have eaten before or since.

SPECKLED CRAB

A speckled crab is similar to a blue claw, except the shell is not as hard. They usually show up on the end of your line while you are surf fishing. There are no size or creel limits on speckled crabs so you can use all you want for bait.

When I catch a speckled crab the first thing I do is cut it up and put it back on the hook. If there are speckled crabs out there, you can bet there are fish out there that eat speckled crabs. These critters have produced whiting, weakfish, croaker and even the occasional bluefish.

3
FROZEN BAIT

While fresh or live bait is always preferable, there are times when frozen bait is all that is available. Offshore anglers along the mid-Atlantic coast, for example, cannot get live ballyhoo and must use the frozen variety. In most locations frozen squid is the only choice bottom fishermen have. Quite often late-season surf fishermen will be unable to find fresh menhaden or mullet and must resort to fresh-frozen. Flounder fishermen use frozen shiners, smelt and sand eels because these baits do not stay alive in any type of livewell and become soft very quickly when stored in a cooler or refrigerator.

Shopping carefully for frozen bait is just as critical as it is for fresh or live bait. The product must have good color and texture and show no signs of freezer burn. Many frozen baits are packed in vacuum bags that keep the air out and the product safe. These bags are a very good idea for anglers who, at the end of the day, find themselves with fresh bait they could not use. Take the excess home and seal it up at the same time you package your catch.

Thawing out frozen bait should be done carefully. Placing a package of bait in salt water is a good way to get things started, but do not thaw out more bait than you need. Once the bait is soft enough to separate, remove a few pieces and put the rest back on ice. Defrosted bait has a tendency to go soft rather quickly, so the less time between defrosting and fishing, the better.

These marlin release flags were the result of trolling frozen baits.

A frozen spot in bad shape. Note freezer burn and milky eye.

I have used bait that was still frozen. Finger mullet, cigar minnows and other small fish can be cut into bait-sized pieces with a
good knife and careful handling. This is a little dangerous, as the
frozen bait is hard and slippery and the knife is sharp. The hook is
placed in the still-frozen bait, which will thaw in the warm water.

Some frozen bait is treated with chemicals before packaging.
Ballyhoo is one example, and the resulting product is much tougher
than it would be if left in its natural state. This toughness is important when trolling the bait at 6 or 7 knots. For some reason the
chemicals do not seem to detract from the bait's ability to attract fish.

SQUID

While it is possible to purchase fresh squid in a few specialty shops,
most anglers fish with the frozen variety. Squid is caught by commercial trawlers and frozen into large blocks. Distributors and some
tackle shops purchase the blocks of squid and repackage them into
smaller quantities. It is also possible to buy already-cleaned squid mantles that are flash frozen and sold by the pound. As you would expect,
they do cost considerably more than a pound of uncleaned product.

Squid comes in various sizes. There are the small ones sold in
tackle shops and grocery stores. The big ones are sold for offshore
trolling and the previously mentioned cleaned mantles. The small
squid are the least expensive, and are great for most bottom fishing
situations. The cleaned mantles are much thicker than the small
squid and work great as strip baits. The big squid are often fished
whole and rigged for tuna and marlin. The largest blue marlin I ever
hooked was on a big squid. Notice I said hooked, not landed.

The small, whole squid are usually cleaned before use. I begin
this project by cutting off the head, removing the skin and splitting
the body or mantle open. Inside there will be some black ink and
a clear, plastic-like piece of cartilage that must be removed. If the
body has any yellow spots or other signs of damage it should be
discarded.

Joe Walker caught this 13-pound flounder on a strip bait.

A strip of squid behind a green hair teaser.

With the clean mantle spread out on the cutting board, I cut it into strips or small sections depending on the target species. Strips are good for flounder and trout. These long, triangle shaped baits are thin and will move in the lightest current, adding to their attraction. A squid-sweetened bucktail has caught many flounder in the surf and from a boat.

Small pieces are used when fish like croaker are the target. Nibblers such as these will chew on a strip forever before getting anywhere near the hook. Keep the bait small and do not let it extend past the barb. You want the bait in the fish's mouth when you feel the bite.

After cleaning a box of squid there will be a pile of squid heads on the cutting board. These make great baits and should never be discarded. Hooked so the tentacles stream out behind the bait, a squid head is a sure thing to draw a strike.

Squid cut open with insides exposed.

Squid cut into strips.

Squid strips on bucktail and plastic squid.

Another use for squid tentacles is as a replacement for worms when fishing for spot or other small fish. When I first heard of this idea I went to the trouble of dyeing the squid tentacles red so they would look like bloodworms. I soon gave up on that process (something about the accidental spill of red food dye in the kitchen), and started fishing with white baits. The fish did not seem to mind. I have caught spot, croaker, kings and even small weakfish on these little baits.

The tentacles are very tough and will remain on the hook for a long time. I thread one at a time on a Chestertown hook, leaving just a little tail hanging behind.

Fishing a small squid whole is a good technique when trying to catch larger flounder, sea bass and weakfish. The whole squid may be fished on a single hook or on a double-hook rig. The double hook setup is often used when flounder fishing, because these fish generally strike from the rear.

The double hook rig is made by snelling two hooks on the same leader. The lead hook is usually adjustable so that the rig can be tailored for baits of various sizes. When used with a whole squid, the lead hook is placed at the pointy end of the squid and the trailer hook is put in the head. The lead hook is adjusted so the squid is straight and not bunched up. The hook can change position while fishing, and will need to be checked and corrected as needed.

I have fished whole squid on a 3 to 6-ounce bucktail when working deep water or in a strong current. The weight of the bucktail gets the bait in the strike zone without the addition of a heavy sinker. Since the introduction of braided line, fishing in this situation is easier because braid is much thinner and more sensitive than mono of the same pound test. A thinner line means less resistance to the water, so the bait can find the bottom with less weight.

Big flounder will hang out in some very rough neighborhoods and the only way to get their attention is with a large bait dropped

Hook squid through top of mantle.

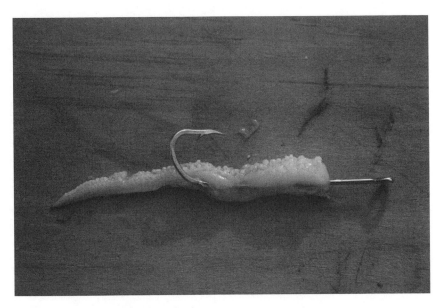

Squid tentacle on a Chestertown hook.

right where they live. The bucktail and whole squid rig works very well in this situation as the angler drifts and vertical jigs over the structure or anchors, and fishes by casting and retrieving the bucktail. In either case, there will be a few rigs lost for every big flounder landed.

The cleaned mantles make excellent baits when cut into long strips. The strips can be placed behind a bucktail or other jig, fished along with a live bait to add more attraction or used alone on a single or double hook rig. The strips will be thicker and longer than ones cut from small squid and tend to stay on the hook after a missed attack.

Squid must be white and when it becomes dirty due to contact with the bottom it must be discarded. Keep a supply of fresh strips ready and do not hesitate to replace a bait when needed.

Whole squid are easy to rig for offshore fishing. A mono or wire leader is run in from the bottom of the mantle and out the top (the

Whole squid on a ball jig.

pointy end). The hook on the end of the leader is set in the head, while an egg sinker or float is used in the mantle to keep the squid from sliding down the leader. When trolled this rig looks exactly like a big squid trying to escape from a predator. Rigged squids are available from shops that specialize in offshore fishing.

SPANISH MACKEREL

Spanish mackerel are a very popular bait for offshore fishing. Some anglers will catch their own, while most purchase the bait frozen. When caught the mackerel must be put immediately into a salt brine to kill it and make it tough. The frozen product is already treated with chemicals to help it withstand trolling speeds.

Rigging a Spanish mackerel involves a good bit of sewing to hold the hook in place and to prevent the body cavity from opening under the pressure of trolling. Experienced mates can do this in a reasonably short time, while the rest of us are better off buying the product already rigged.

SWIMMING MULLET

The swimming mullet is another offshore bait that requires a bit of work and practice to get right. First, the backbone of the mullet must be removed by running a boning tool down the spine from the head to the tail. This tool is a hollow rod and when done correctly it will completely remove the backbone and leave the bait as limp as a dishrag.

Next a filet knife is inserted about two-thirds of the way between the head and the tail. Care must be taken to keep the knife from slicing the bait in half as it is run to and through the tail. The finished product will have the tail split perfectly in half.

The hook is placed through the mouth and out the stomach before the leader is attached.

When I was fishing offshore several days a week I could count on one in two of my swimming mullet to actually swim, and I was tying them on dry land the evening before the trip. During an excursion with a real captain and mate, I watched as the mate tied a dozen swimming mullet on the run out with the deck pitching and rolling. Needless to say every one of his baits swam as if it were alive.

BALLYHOO

The most popular bait for offshore fishing is the ballyhoo. Available as live or fresh bait in southern locations, it is sold as a frozen product north of the Florida Keys.

There are several sizes of ballyhoo, from small to large to horse. The smaller ones are used to attract white marlin, while the bigger ones are set out in hopes of attracting blue marlin, bigeye and bluefin tuna.

Ballyhoo are rigged as skip baits and swimming baits. The difference is that the swimming baits have a small egg sinker located under the chin, while the skip baits do not carry any extra weight.

Ballyhoo are rigged by putting the hook in the gill plates and then out through the anus. This requires sliding the bait on the hook until the point is located correctly. At this point the hook is secured

Prepackaged and prerigged ballyhoo, swimming mullet, and squid.

to the bait with copper rigging wire, and if a sinker is to be added it is put on now.

New federal regulations require all marlin tournaments to use only circle hooks on dead baits. Rather than placing the hook inside the ballyhoo it is secured to the outside of the head. This is not the best location for tuna and dolphin, but the results with marlin and sailfish have been good.

CIGAR MINNOWS

Cigar minnows are usually sold in boxes with the baits frozen inside. The fish are about 3 to 4 inches long and, as you might have guessed, shaped a little like a cigar.

Cigar minnows can be used with a king mackerel live bait rig or cut up and fished in pieces. I was surprised to find that cigar minnows would catch king mackerel after having been told that live bait, preferably bunker, was the only thing a king would eat. On the day this great secret was revealed to me we caught the kings on cigar minnows, and used the rest of the box as chum by cutting the minnows into pieces and dropping them in the water behind the boat.

Cigar minnows are also used whole when bottom fishing for snapper and grouper. On a head boat trip out of Sarasota, Florida the captain advised us to purchase a box or two of minnows, as these were the best baits for the area where we would be fishing. I figured this was a ploy to drive up more business for the mates who sold the bait, but I had to have a box before we left the dock.

Once on site the cigar minnows outfished the cut squid supplied by the boat by a wide margin. I caught bluefish, grouper, vermillion snappers and banded rudderfish using those cigar minnows. At first I was fishing with a whole bait, but it did not take long for the bluefish to show me the error of my ways. Cutting the cigar minnows into thirds worked just fine.

SHINERS

Shiners are sold frozen in small packages and are fished whole with two or three on the hook. Never thaw out more than you need, because this bait turns into mush in a very short time.

Frozen shiners on a flounder rig. Always use two or three baits on the hook.

I have caught shiners in a haul seine and tried to keep them alive without success. The best I could do was keep some of them fresh for use that day and freeze the rest.

Summer flounder are the primary target for anglers fishing with shiners. Two or more shiners are used at the same time by hooking them through the eyes. Since the bait is so soft, it is easily removed, so bait checks must be made every few minutes. As with all flounder baits, a slight dropback must be used when a fish is felt on the line.

Strange as it may seem, I have had times when a soft, dead, half-frozen shiner outfished live minnows. I never go flounder fishing without a bag or two of frozen shiners in my cooler.

SMELT

Smelt are a northern fish that is caught for food and sport in New England. My only association with them has been as a baitfish used for summer flounder.

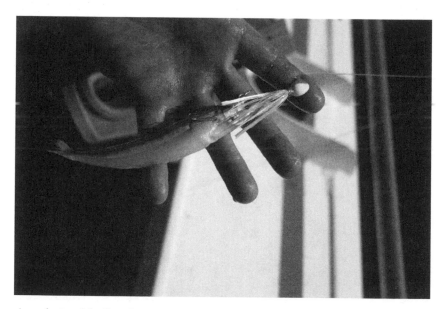

A smelt rigged for flounder.

This flounder fell for a smelt.

Smelt are usually fished whole with a double hook rig. They are fairly tough for a frozen bait and do well even when the water is warm.

With the minimum size limit for summer flounder growing so large in recent years, big baits such as smelt have become popular. The idea is a larger bait attracts a larger class of flounder, and for the most part the theory is a sound one. Exactly why a summer flounder in Virginia that has never crossed paths with a smelt would find one so appealing is something I do not pretend to understand.

BUTTERFISH

Believe it or not, when I was a kid we ate butterfish. My grandfather purchased them from the market and fried them up for dinner. If my memory serves, and it seldom does, these were fresh fish, but they could have been frozen and then thawed before sale.

Today butterfish are usually purchased in 25-pound flats and used as chum and bait for tuna. Most of the time the butterfish will be chopped up on the way out to the grounds by the mate, with some help from the crew if they are active participants and not just along for the ride.

My longtime friend and charter captain John Nedelka invented and holds the patent for a machine that makes this job easier and safer. Aptly called Captain John's Chunking Machine, it works by cutting three or four butterfish at a time into perfect sized chunks. Equipped with stainless steel blades, the machine opens up to allow the bait to be placed on the cutting area. When closed, the blades cut the bunker and the chunks fall into a five-gallon bucket placed below.

Cutting by hand involves sharp knives, slippery fish and a moving target as the boat rocks and rolls. Cuts are common, and self-inflicted amputations are not unheard of.

When I ran a 24-foot Albemarle, the cockpit space was too small for cutting baits on the way to the grounds. I cut the bait up the night before the trip and stored the chunks in a cooler well-packed with ice.

Whole butterfish are often used as bait when chunking for tuna. The hook is put in the mouth and out the gill opening before being buried in the side of the fish, where it is concealed from the tuna. There will be hot bites, when everything that hits the water is taken by a tuna, but in a more common situation the tuna is very picky, and will only take a well-presented bait. Fooling a tuna in this scenario requires a very stealthy presentation where the bait must look natural, with no hook showing, and the leader may have to be as light as 20 or 30-pound test.

A leader that light will not last long in the jaw of a 100-pound tuna, so anglers have devised a rig that drops a plastic tube down the line to the hook after the tuna takes the bait. Sometimes called a tuna bomb, the tube is held up the line by a rubber band that releases when the weight of the tuna causes the line to come tight. In theory, the tube will fall down the line and lodge in the tuna's mouth, acting as chafing gear to keep the line from parting. Like a lot of other good ideas, sometimes it works and sometimes it does not.

4

ARTIFICIAL BAIT

One invention that has changed fishing with bait like nothing else in the history of the sport is the development of artificial bait. Not only do these baits look like the real thing, they smell and taste just like it too.

BERKLEY

As is often the case, the first successful artificial baits were produced for the freshwater bass fishermen. Berkley had the Power Bait product on the market for several years while developing Gulp! Berkley scientists Dr. Keith Jones, a fish biologist and John Prochnow, a chemist, spent 20 years in the lab before they thought the product was ready for the market.

So what is the difference between Gulp! and Power Bait? Power Bait is made from PVC plastic and an oil-based resin, while Gulp! is made with a water-based resin. With an oil-based resin the scent is trapped in the bait until a fish bites. With a water-based resin the scent begins to disperse as soon as the bait hits the water.

Mr. Prochnow recommends using a Power Bait until it falls off the hook. The more bites and nicks the bait has, the more scent it releases.

Gulp! crab used to catch sea bass.

Croaker caught on a Gulp! crab.

The Gulp! product should be fished slow and easy, as the constantly released scent leaves a trail that a fish will follow long before he actually sees the bait. Add to this the taste the fish experiences when he does bite the Gulp!, and it easy to see why this product works so well.

Gulp! gets it scent from the liquid it is packaged in. This may be in the bottom of the bag or in a bucket of Gulp! Alive. This is the first layer of scent; there are two more. The second is what science has discovered is attractive to all fish. The third layer contains the scent of that particular bait, be it shrimp, bunker, eel or crab.

Mr. Prochnow says a Gulp! bait can be fished all day and still retain more scent that any other bait, but he will change his out after an hour. The used bait goes back in the bag or Gulp! Alive bucket to rejuvenate, and in about an hour it is ready to go again.

Gulp! will keep for a long time in the original bag and even longer in the Gulp! Alive bucket. This is better than natural bait that

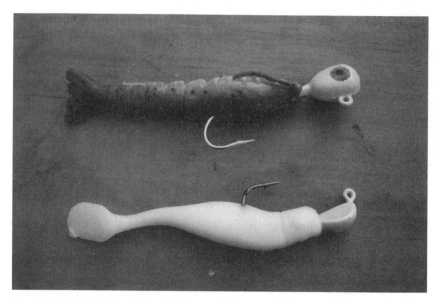

Top, Gulp! Shrimp on a jig head. Bottom, FishBites Shad on a jig head.

must be frozen or thrown away after a day of fishing. The bait needs no refrigeration and while it is not a good idea to leave it exposed to the hot sun, it will survive for a while even in those harsh conditions.

One word of warning. Gulp! left on the hook until it dries is very difficult to remove. The process requires a sharp knife, careful work and a bit of patience.

FISHBITES

The other artificial bait on the market is the product of one man's interest in chemistry and marine biology. Dr. William Carr realized at an early age that chemicals leaking from fresh-cut bait attracted fish and stimulated them to feed. Called feeding stimulants, these chemicals were later identified by Dr. Carr during his graduate work at Duke University. His first work was with shrimp, where he isolated several stimulants. He then identified even more from baits such as crab, clam, squid, crawfish, bloodworm, and others.

The author caught this triggerfish on a Fishbites clam.

Analyses of these diverse bait types provided a series of proprietary mixtures of natural chemicals that were combined with a soft, flesh-like material to produce synthetic baits called Fishbites.

One type of Fishbites is made from the flesh-like sheets of various thickness, flavor, texture, and color. The sheets are cut into bait-size portions by the angler. In the water Fishbites gradually soften and dissolve, releasing feeding stimulants throughout the water and in the fish's mouth. A thin layer of tear-resistant fabric in each bait keeps it on the hook much longer than most natural baits.

Fishbites are all bait, with no guts, scales or other parts to discard. Cut into any size or shape they can be used on a hook for bottom fishing or as a trailing bait on a jig or spoon.

The Fishbites Bloodworm Alternative has been a revolution in the northeast. Bloodworms are expensive with a short shelf life. The Fishbites product works as well as the real thing, lasts forever in its package and remains on the hook for a longer

FishBites clam on small circle hooks. Note fabric between layers to hold bait on the hook.

period of time. I have used this product with great success on kings, spot and croaker.

Fishbites Xtreme is the latest product in the line. Instead of sheets, Xtreme baits are molded into shapes designed to fish on jig heads or weighted hooks, and imitate the action of live bait. Unlike sheet baits that dissolve in water, Xtreme baits are designed to maintain their shape while constantly releasing scent for an extended period of time.

5

TOOLS OF THE TRADE

As with any type of fishing, the angler needs certain tools to do the job properly. To save repetition, let me say at the beginning that any tools, tackle, line or hooks must be of the highest quality. Nothing ensures failure surer than poor equipment.

High quality does not always mean high cost. Good, sturdy tackle will always cost more than bad, weak junk, but the investment will pay big dividends.

In today's fishing market there are spinning reels that cost over $1,000 and should stand up to the largest fish in the ocean. High-quality spinning reels are available at one third the cost, and will handle all the fish most of us are likely to catch. The same is true with all tackle; there are reasonably priced items that will perform as well as the over-the-top stuff that is reserved for folks with more money than I will ever have.

RODS AND REELS

Fishing with bait is done using every type of rod and reel ever invented. The angler needs to choose the outfit that best suits his current fishing situation. The idea that one rod and reel can be used for all types of fishing is a falsehood started by a disgruntled wife when her husband wanted to buy some new tackle.

This flounder hit a Tsunami ball jig sweetened with a strip of squid.

Spinning outfits should be used when light baits are cast. Tossing pinfish to snook lurking in the mangroves is a good example of this type of fishing.

Long range boats in the Pacific use small live baits to fish for very big tuna. In this case a rod with a soft tip and a powerful butt is required. The rod is shorter than a similar trolling rod, and is used with a stand-up harness. The conventional reel matched with this rod can cast a light bait without a backlash and retains the power and smooth drag required to fight a tuna.

On the east coast tuna rods are sturdy sticks that can put plenty of pressure on the fish. Even when chunking, the heavier rods are used, with more and more anglers going for the shorter stand-up sticks in this application. Reels such as the Penn International or Diawa Sealine Tournament are often used for tuna chunking. I use

A sturdy rod and reel is required to pull a tog from its lair. A good set of foul weather gear keeps the angler warm and dry.

Penn Senators and the regular Diawa Sealines, because they are much less expensive and will land any tuna that I am likely to hook.

Bottom fishing for sea bass, tog, croaker and similar fish may require the use of a heavy weight to put the bait in the strike zone. While the target fish could be handled by light tackle, the weight of the sinker requires something with more backbone.

It is common for 8- to 10-ounce sinkers to be used when bottom fishing, so the rod must be rated to hold that much lead. A lighter rod will collapse under the weight, making it difficult to detect a bite and putting the rod on the edge of breaking.

My favorite bottom fishing outfit is a Berkley Lightning rod (LRC761H) matched to an Ambassadeur 7000iHSN reel filled with 30-pound Stren braid. This set will work with sinkers up to 6 ounces. When more weight is needed, I use a custom-made rod with a tip the size of a pool cue that has a Penn Jig Master reel filled with 40-pound Stren braid. This outfit has wrestled up some very determined tog from over 100 feet of water.

Every region of the country has special rod and reel combos used for a fishery that is particular to that area. In the north it may be live-lining for stripers. In the south it is live bait trolling for kings, and in the northwest it is mooching for salmon.

When in doubt, check with your local tackle shop for guidance. These guys and gals have the experience to steer you in the right direction. The clerk in the big box store, if you can find one, may have been in ladies undergarments yesterday and does not know anything about fishing. I have seen customers leave these stores with spinning reels on conventional rods and vice versa. Having managed a tackle shop, I know that the prices are cheaper in a big box store, but the service at your local shop is worth more than the few bucks saved in a place where nobody knows your name.

LINES

Fishing lines have come a long way since the days when my grand-father used linen line to catch his croaker and trout. That line had to be removed from the reel after each trip, soaked in fresh water and then cranked on a drying rack. Once dry, the line was put back on the reel. I have several of his rods and reels hanging on the wall in my office, where they will remain.

In the 1950s DuPont marketed the first successful nylon fishing line, and no one has used linen line since. No one, that is, except my grandfather, who back in 1974 outfished my brother, my step-father and me on a foggy day in Delaware. He caught more flounder than the three of us combined using linen line, cat gut leaders and a brass flounder rig. Perhaps the old saying that the skill of the angler is more important than his equipment holds some truth.

Nylon monofilament fishing line has many good points, and a few that are not so good. It is tough, smooth, ties strong knots and will lie on the reel without kinking up. On the other hand, it absorbs water, which makes it weaker. Mono also has a certain amount of stretch, which can be a blessing and a curse. When fighting a big fish close to the boat, that stretch provides a shock absorber, keeping the action of the fish from breaking the line or pulling out the hook. When trying to set the hook with a few hundred feet of line in the water, stretch can cause some difficulty. Sunlight is another problem for mono lines, as the UV rays cause it to become brittle and weak.

Then along came the new breed of braided lines. The first products had the abrasion resistance of wet toilet paper and would wear out after a few days on the water. Improvements were soon made and the products available in today's market are durable.

Braided line does not stretch and is much thinner than a similar pound-test mono line. These properties allow the angler to get deep with less weight and to feel a fish who is just thinking about biting. Braided line seems to me to be more prone to wind knots than mono.

When using braided line most anglers choose a pound-test rating that is heavier than they would use with mono. This is fine, so long as the heavier pound-test is considered when setting the drag. Since the line will take a much heavier weight it may seem like a good idea to crank the drag down and put maximum pressure on the fish. Unfortunately, the rod may be rated for a much lighter pound-test and could break under the added pressure. I have also found a lighter drag setting is beneficial when the fish is close to the net or gaff. A sudden lunge for freedom can be successful for the fish if the lack of stretch in the braided line causes another component of the system to fail.

I do use braided line on all my bottom fishing and casting outfits. The advantages of braid are just too significant to be overlooked. I still keep mono on my trolling rigs, because the stretch will act to cushion the force of the strike and protect my equipment.

All of my braid-filled reels have a mono shock leader. In the surf I use 50-pound line tied to the braid with an Albright knot and wrapped around the reel spool three to four times. Bottom fishing reels have the same 50-pound line, but only five or six feet long. Lighter casting outfits will have leaders that vary between 20 and 50-pound test.

While new braided lines have much better abrasion resistance than the original product, I still think mono has more. The knots needed to connect braid to a rig are new to me (old dogs, new tricks) so I prefer to use the same mono knots I have employed since childhood. Finally, mono is less visible in the water than braid, so I like it tied to my rig.

LURES AND BAIT

Throughout the book we have mentioned several situations where bait and lures are combined to add more attraction to both. A lure possesses color and motion, while a bait will have an alluring scent.

The jig and bait is the most common combination used in salt water. Jigs come in any number of types and sizes, from $\frac{1}{16}$-ounce to several pounds. Believe it or not, but those tiny $\frac{1}{16}$-ounce crappie jigs when combined with a small, thin strip of squid will catch a decent-

A variety of lures that can be sweetened with bait.

sized flounder, and the same jig used with grass shrimp will pull white perch out of tidal creeks.

A 1-ounce white bucktail matched to a strip of dog shark belly will catch all the flounder you want out of the surf. The same bucktail and a chunk of peeler crab will draw weakfish from far and near.

Take a dead eel, hook it on a swimming jig, and it will come back to life. A dead mullet fished on a jig and bounced along the bottom has much more life than the same bait drifting along on a top-bottom rig.

Hardly a bait goes overboard behind an offshore trolling boat without some sort of lure in front to make it more attractive and keep it from washing out. It may be an expensive Ilander or an inexpensive Sea Witch, but in most situations the lure will draw more strikes than a naked bait.

Shark fishermen often drape a rubber skirt over a whole or filet bait to add more action. Most shark fishing is done from a drifting boat, so the bait just hangs there. The skirt will move as the boat rocks in even the smallest waves, making the bait more attractive.

The color of the lure is important, but we never know for sure what color is going to be important on any given day. It is generally accepted that fish do not perceive color the way humans do. Fish are more sensitive to contrast than to color. This means that a bright lure against a dark background is going to draw the fish's attention no matter the color of the bright lure. The opposite is also true, and a dark lure will stand out against a bright background. This is why a black lure works so well at night. The very light-sensitive eye of the fish sees the night sky as bright, and the black lure stands out in contrast.

In deep water most light is filtered out. I have found white or chartreuse-colored feathers and hair attract more attention from bottom dwellers than a plain hook. In really deep water a glow stick can add some light. This setup is commonly used when fishing for swordfish with whole squid in depths over 1,000 feet.

Lures that reflect light can be used with bait. Decorating a top-bottom rig by using a small spoon instead of the hook and baiting with a thin strip of cut fish will pull in bluefish, flounder, trout and the occasional Spanish mackerel. This rig will work from a boat or from the surf.

Spoons can also be trolled or cast with a strip of bait attached. The bait slows down the action of the spoon while adding an alluring tail that redfish find irresistible. Squid and filets of fish are the most popular additions to a spoon. Cut long, thin strips for maximum action.

Colored floats are a popular decoration in the surf. Some anglers believe the floats keep the bait away from the crabs. I have tossed away numerous floats after they were cut in two by crab claws to disprove that theory. The floats do add action and color to the bait, and some protection to the leader from sharp teeth.

Bottom fishermen frequently add spinner blades, beads and floats to their hooks. These additions create noise and help attract fish when the water is dirty. Since sound travels much better underwater than light, fish often locate a meal by hearing it long before they actually see or smell the bait. Between its lateral line and its inner ear, a fish can home in on its prey from quite a distance.

The only end to the number of ways bait and lures can be combined is the imagination of the angler. And we all know most fishermen have a vivid imagination.

CAST NETS AND HAUL SEINES

Cast Nets

The only way to become proficient with is cast net is the same way you get to Carnegie Hall—practice, practice, practice. Begin with a small model and once you become reasonably proficient with it, you can move up to the larger versions. The best place to practice throwing a cast net is from the end of a pier. This will allow you to become confident in your throwing ability before attempting a cast from the bow of a moving boat.

Cast nets come in different diameters with various mesh sizes and sinker weights. A six- to eight-foot net is a good starting point. Select the mesh size to match the bait you plan to target—larger mesh for bunker, smaller for anchovies or finger mullet. The heavier the weight, the faster the net will sink. A fast-sinking net is more likely to trap bait as the fish dive for the bottom to escape. A larger mesh net will sink faster than a small mesh because there is less resistance from the strands to the water.

The mate prepares to throw a cast net.

The net hits the water.

A cast net has several parts. The net itself should be made from a soft monofilament so it will open to its full width. A limp net is also easier to load and throw. The net is divided into panels that should lay flat on the floor without a cone rising up in the middle.

Braille lines connect to the lead line on the bottom of the net. These lines pull the net inward, trapping all the bait in the net.

The horn of the net is the device that keeps the Braille lines separated. The best horns are divided into four parts, equally dividing the Braille lines and preventing tangles.

The lead weights on a cast net are located on the bottom and are held in place by a heavy line. The line and the weights are secured to the net by tying off on every mesh section. The better quality nets have the weights spaced close to each other.

Different states have different laws regarding the use of cast nets. Be sure to check with the local authorities before using a cast net in any body of water, salt or fresh.

A net full of bait.

The Cast

The following instructions are taken from the website of Black Pearl Cast Nets, castnetworld.com. This company offers a video, "The Art of Castnet Throwing," which I recommend since many of us have trouble relating the written word into action.

STEP 1   Slip the castnet throw line through the hand loop and tighten around your throwing arm.

STEP 2   Coil the throw line into neat, loose loops into your castnet throwing hand.

STEP 3   Grasp the castnet ring palm down. Fingers on top, thumb on bottom.

STEP 4   With your free hand, reach straight down from your thumb and grasp the lead line.

STEP 5   Place that section of lead line into your palm. The castnet ring will hold it in place.

STEP 6   Turn your palm down and you are ready to throw your cast net.

STEP 7   Rotate the castnet a full ¾-turn away from your target.

STEP 8   With your throwing arm outstretched, rotate in a smooth, continuous motion toward your target.

STEP 9   Release the castnet into the air at a slight upward angle in the direction of your live bait target.

STEP 10   The castnet should hit the water in a circular form.

STEP 11   Let the castnet sink to your desired depth, and pull the throw-line to close the net.

Haul Seines

A haul seine is a net that is stretched between two poles and pulled through the water by two operators. One person stands on the beach, while the other wades out directly in front of the first. Should the water depth exceed the height of the second person as he or she wades out, it is a good idea to change course and walk parallel to the beach until the net has reached its full length. At this point the person in the water walks towards the beach, while keeping the bottom of the net in constant contact with the bottom of the bay or whatever body of water he is fishing. If the bottom of the net is allowed to rise up above the bottom of the bay, fish will escape and the person on the beach will become quite agitated.

Once the person in the water reaches land, he and the anchor man on the beach will move towards each other, dragging the net ashore. At this point there will be all sorts of critters in the net and for some reason, only the ones you want for bait will be jumping out. Mullet, silversides, spot and minnows will be heading for the water while skates, dog sharks, jellyfish and crabs will be all but impossible to dislodge.

If there are any small children around they can be employed to catch the escaping bait. I was blessed with two sons that I always took with me when using a haul seine.

Haul seines should only be used in calm, shallow water. I once tried to use a haul seine in the ocean and even though it was a relatively calm day, I was tossed around like a leaf in the wind.

A haul seine can be purchased in various lengths and mesh sizes. Something less than 100 feet long is more than enough for two part-time netters to handle. Select the mesh size that best fits the target bait.

As with the cast net, the use of a haul seine is often governed by state laws. The operator may need a license, or there may be restrictions on the length and mesh size allowed for private use. Check with your local authorities before buying a haul seine.

HOOKS AND SINKERS

Hooks

The variety of hooks available to fishermen is worthy of a separate book, so we will only discuss the most popular ones used by salt-water bait fishermen.

Circle hooks have to be at the top of the list because they are easy to use, are seldom swallowed by fish, and hold in place very well. First used by long-line commercial fishermen because they set themselves without any help, circle hooks became popular with recreational fishermen about 20 years ago.

My introduction to circle hooks came in 1989 during an amberjack trip with the late Dr. Jim Wright out of Virginia Beach, Virginia. We were fishing from Captain Dave Wright's boat, High

The author's box of hooks, snaps and swivels.

Hopes and had run 50 miles south to what they called the South Tower. This is an impressive tower in 20 fathoms used by the Navy to train fighter pilots, and is home to thousands of amberjack during the summer.

When Dr. Wright showed me a circle hook I thought he was nuts. How could a hook that bent back on its self catch anything? Well, it caught everything. The procedure was to drop a hapless live croaker or spot alongside the tower and watch as it was engulfed by an amberjack. The jack was allowed to swim off a short distance before the lever drag was placed in the strike position. When the line came tight the jack was hooked, every time. To prevent the jack from getting into the tower, Captain Wright would put the High Hopes in gear and power away. For those who have never hooked a 40- to 50-pound amberjack, let me say the combination of the jack trying to swim to the tower and the boat pulling away from the tower made for some excitement as the angler tried to stay aboard while all the forces of nature tried to pull him overboard.

Since that first introduction, I have gradually switched almost all of my hooks to circles. So far I have found nothing they won't catch, and they consistently provide a better hook-up ratio than J hooks.

One fish that does not seem to fall to circle hooks any better than to J hooks is the tog. When you watch how they eat it becomes clear why the circle is not more effective. A tog takes the bait in its mouth and crushes it. He then swallows the meat and spits out the shell and the hook. The circle hook never gets inside the tog's mouth, where it can do its work. Triggerfish and sheepshead have the same eating habits.

The circle hooks works by following the inside of a fish's mouth until it lodges in the corner or hinge. Even when the bait is swallowed, the hook will never lodge in the stomach because it rides out on its round side until it turns and hooks the fish in the mouth.

For those of us who grew up fishing with J hooks, it can take a little training to learn how to fish with a circle hook. The hardest thing to master is not setting the hook when the fish first hits the bait. The angler must drop back and let the fish get the hook inside its mouth before coming tight on the line. A hard hook set is not needed; just let the line come tight and the fish will be hooked.

Even when fishing for croaker, I let the line go slack by dropping the rod tip at the first hint of a bite, and when I raise the rod back up the fish is hooked. The same tactic works with flounder, sea bass and most other bottom fish.

Most of my surf fishing is done with the rod in a sand spike. This technique was made for circle hooks. By the time I pull my fat butt out of the beach chair and get to the rod, the fish is hooked.

I still use J hooks for some applications. The long-shanked Chestertown hook is ideal for fishing with worms or squid tentacles. The spot and whiting that I target with these baits have small, under-slung mouths and suck a bait up off the bottom. The long, thin hook allows me to thread the worm on and the fish to suck hook and bait at the same time.

The Virginia-style hook is a favorite with tog fishermen. As mentioned earlier, circle hooks are not much of an advantage when fishing for tog, while Virginia hooks are strong and sharp, making for a quick penetration of those tough tog lips. They also have the power not to break or straighten out under the pressure of convincing a tog to leave his lair.

I try to avoid treble hooks, but in a few applications they are necessary. One such application is live bait trolling for king mackerel. As previously mentioned, the idea is to snag the fish, not hook it in the mouth, so the more barbs the better.

Unfortunately, I have seen trebles used in baits intended for flounder and striped bass. This is a bad idea because both species have a high minimum size limit, making it likely a short fish will be caught. The treble hook is often swallowed, and this results in a dead striper or flounder that no one can keep. Please, use only circle hooks when fishing for any species with a minimum size to reduce the catch-and-release mortality.

Sinkers

Sinkers come in as many sizes and styles as hooks. The bank sinker is one of the most popular styles when the angler wants the bait to move over the bottom. Its rounded, tear-drop shape will glide smoothly over sand or mud when drifting from a boat or casting from the shore or a bridge.

Surf sinkers are traditionally shaped like a triangle, with a flat top and sharply angled sides. Called pyramid sinkers, they dig into the sand and hold the rig in place.

A variation of this model, known as the Hatteras sinker, has the same triangle top, but the body is rounded. The rounded body is supposed to be more aerodynamic and will cast further. My casting

A selection of surf sinkers.

skills are not to the level that I can tell the difference between the two.

A surf sinker with several wires protruding will cast very well and hold like glue when the wires deploy. This is a favorite when the rig must be cast a long distance. The sinker is tapered at both ends so it will have very little resistance to the air, and the wires are used to dig into the sand and hold bottom. At times the wires hold so well it can be chore to get them back out.

The tongue sinker is shaped like its namesake, with a concave opening on the wide end. It does cast very well and when that opening digs into the sand, the rig will be anchored in place.

The rubber core sinker is used when weight must be changed frequently to compensate for changing depths and currents. The sinker is quick and easy to add to the line and with the rubber core, chafing is held to a minimum. When used while fishing live bait, the rubber core sinker is attached to the point where the leader joins the line. In this position it still drops the bait to the desired depth, but does not dampen its action.

Spadefish are notorious for feeding at one depth and ignoring baits set at any other level. Sad to say, but spades do not announce their feeding level at the start of the day, so the angler must find out for himself. Setting clam baits at various depths behind the boat using rubber core sinkers below a bobber is the most practical method for solving this mystery. Once the magic depth is located it is easy to put the same weight rubber core sinkers on all lines.

Split shots are used in much the same way as rubber core sinkers. They are crimped to the line or leader when just the slightest amount of extra weight is required. Normally used with small baits such as grass shrimp, split shots can be added just above the hook like a very small jig.

Egg sinkers can be used like fish-finders by passing the running line through the hole before tying on the hook and leader. Putting a chafing tube in the hole can prevent line wear. This rig is used most often when a small weight is needed to get the bait down to the strike zone. I have used it in shallow water to put a minnow on the bottom for flounder or a mole crab for kingfish. The rig is cast and slowly retrieved.

There are a few special sinkers that are used when fishing over rocks or wrecks. Most of the time this rubble will eat sinkers because the weights fall into a hole or crack and become wedged. Wreck sinkers are flat and very thin. The theory is a thin sinker will come out of a hole or crack much easier than a big, fat bank sinker. Some of these sinkers are round like a coin, while others are long like a pencil. I have used both styles, got some back, and lost others.

There are special types of sinkers used all along the coast to target certain fish or to overcome certain fishing situations. If a local guide tells you to use a sinker you have never seen before, don't argue. Tie it on exactly the way he tells you and start catching fish.

SCISSORS

A good pair of scissors can be a big help when preparing bait. I use them to cut crabs, worms, squid and lots of other stuff. In many situations a pair of scissors can cut bait quicker and safer than a knife.

You will find high-quality scissors hanging on the wall in most tackle shops. These are fine instruments in a very nice case or sheath. They can cut braided line, mono or Fluorocarbon leader, and in some cases, braided wire. These are not bait scissors.

Chicken farming is a popular industry in my part of the world and the processing plants go through thousands of scissors every month. Enterprising businessmen collect these scissors, refurbish and resell them to fishermen. These are bait scissors. I have seen them on sale in New Jersey and New York, where chicken houses are few and far between. If you can't find chicken scissors in your tackle shop, go to a department store and buy the cheapest pair of kitchen shears you can find.

Cutting crabs with a knife is sloppy at best and dangerous at worst. With a pair of bait scissors, simply hold the crab in one hand and cut it in half down the middle. Then cut each half in half or in quarters. Quick, easy and safe.

Want to cut squid into strips? Snip, snip, snip and the job is done. I have even cut frozen finger mullet into chunks with a pair of scissors.

As with any tool used near saltwater, a little maintenance goes a long way. Give the scissors a good spray of WD-40 after each trip and they will outlive you.

PLIERS

Fishing pliers come in many shapes, sizes and prices. Over the years I used several types and have settled on three models. I carry a pair of Donnmar pliers on my belt and a pair of X-Tools in my fishing bag. I find the Donnmar pliers to be light yet strong, while the X-Tools will cut braid and float. I cannot get used to the almost weightless feeling of the X-Tools when removing the hook from a big fish.

My first pair of pliers were Manleys and they were very heavy. When carried on my belt they felt like they were pulling my pants down, a sight no one should see. Over the years I used them on everything from spot to giant bluefin. The only problem I had was that the blades would wear out and could not be replaced.

After the blades were shot I would keep on using and cussing that pair of pliers until I lost them or threw them overboard. Finally, I shot the lock off my wallet and bought the Donnmars. I have been carrying them on my belt for 10 years. The blades are still fine and my pants stay up. If and when the blades do wear out, I know I can replace them.

My pair of Manleys now resides in my surf fishing tackle box. I use them to take hooks out of big bluefish, cut wire leaders, and drive nails into solid oak. They must be cleaned with WD-40 after every immersion in saltwater or they will rust shut.

If I only carried one pair of pliers, it would be the Leatherman Wave. This multi-tool has everything an angler needs, including pliers, knives, screwdrivers, scissors, and wire cutters. I never leave the dock or go on the surf without my pair in the tackle bag. The only reason I don't use them as my primary pair of pliers is because it is quicker to get my Donnmars out of the sheath, and as mentioned earlier, the Donnmars are lighter.

I am familiar with anglers who think they are saving money by purchasing inexpensive needle-nose pliers from the local dollar store. This is false economy. The cheap pliers will rust shut almost immediately or break the first time pressure is applied. I have seen their dead bodies rusted shut in the bottom of tackle boxes. If you are going to buy a pair of pliers to take fishing, buy fishing pliers.

KNIVES

It is all but impossible to fish with bait and not use a knife. One knife will not do everything safely, so it is important to have the right knife for the job at hand.

Filet knives are needed to remove the meat from the bone. Filets make great baits because their slim profile allows the current to move them in an enticing manner.

Cutting chunks requires a knife with a strong backbone and a sharp blade. A thin filet knife blade will collapse when used to cut through bone. This often requires a trip to the emergency room for stitches.

All knives must be kept sharp. Take them to a professional knife sharpener at least once a season and keep them sharp at home with croc sticks.

Dexter Russell makes a complete line of fishing knives. I have all of their models and find they do everything from preparing the bait to cleaning the catch. Rapala has a nice little bait knife that is sturdy enough to cut frozen bunker or mullet.

While we all get the occasional cut or puncture wound when handling fish, it is a good idea to wear gloves when cutting or cleaning large amounts of fish. Gloves provide a solid grip on the fish and the knife, as well as protecting the wearer from serous injury should a slip occur.

CUTTING BOARDS

A sturdy cutting board is the working base for preparing bait. While most anything will work when fishing from shore, a solid base is necessary when cutting bait in a moving boat.

A popular style of bait board attaches to the boat using the built-in rod holders. Most models have slots for rigging pliers and knives, as well as an overboard drain to make clean up easier.

For boats without rod holders, the Bucket Board is a good choice. The board slips on the top of a five-gallon bucket and has a lip around the side, with an opening that corresponds to the hole left by the part of the bucket not covered by the board. As the bait is cleaned the waste can be pushed into the hole and collects in the bottom of the bucket. When there is no waste, such as when cutting up bunker for chunks, the chunks can be collected in the bottom of the bucket. The board with cut bait can be removed from the bucket and stored in a cooler.

When fishing from the surf or pier, I have a cutting board purchased at a kitchen store for a few bucks. It fits perfectly on the top of my cooler and is very easy to clean.

It is possible to construct a custom cutting board and I have seen a few with teak sides and other fancy touches. I doubt the cost of building a cutting board is much cheaper than buying one, so I think the builders are more interested in the idea of doing it themselves they way they want it done.

LIVEWELLS

Livewells come in all shapes and sizes to fit any application necessary. The vast majority of boats built since 1990 have a livewell as
standard equipment. While this is the ideal setup, there are plenty of
boats on the water without a livewell.

Fortunately, there is an aftermarket that produces livewells that
fit almost any boat. Some provide only oxygen from an air pump,
while others pump water from outside the boat to the tank then
drain the excess overboard.

My 1988 24 Albemarle did not have a built in livewell so I used
a 30-gallon trashcan with an air pump. This would keep three dozen
spot alive all day. It would not keep bunker alive because they
require a recirculating livewell.

To hook up a recirculating livewell requires a bit of plumbing.
A pump must be installed and a hose run through a through-hull
fitting to the pump, and another hose from the overflow back over-

A large recirculating livewell will keep the bait alive and frisky.

board. This will vary for every boat and the livewell systems are sold with instructions. I do believe it is better to let the overflow go directly overboard and not run down the deck and out the scuppers as I have seen on some boats.

A small net must be used to remove the bait from the livewell. Trying to catch bait with your hands is entertaining for the crew, but is an inefficient method that tends to injure more fish than it catches.

A bait bucket is an easy way to keep small baits alive. It is tossed overboard between uses and the bait swims in fresh, cool water. The bait bucket should be stored in a five-gallon bucket when the boat is moved. The keeps the maximum amount of water in the bucket and keeps the excess out of the boat. Leaving the bucket overboard when moving the boat at speed is an experience most fishermen have enjoyed at least once. Besides giving the bait an exciting ride, this practice often results in the loss of the bucket.

Surf fishermen are pretty much on their own when transporting live bait. So far as I know, no one mass-produces a livewell for a surf fishing vehicle. I made mine many years ago when live spot were used to catch huge weakfish out of the mid-Atlantic surf. In those days you could purchase three-dozen spot for $10.00. Today they cost $2.50 each.

My live well is a large cooler that fits the cooler rack on the front of my truck. It is outfitted with a bilge pump, PVC pipe and a plastic tube. I drilled holes all along the PVC pipe and capped one end. I used the plastic hose to connect the bilge pump to the pipe. The wires from the pump run out of the cooler to the battery. The pipe is hung from the cooler hinges with 50-pound fishing line.

This rig will keep three dozen spot alive all day. I do change out the water using a five-gallon bucket, especially on warm days. It is a good idea to start the truck every half hour or so to keep the battery charged.

I have seen professional bait catchers use an air pump mounted under the hood to keep a hundred or more spot or mullet alive. The air is pumped directly to several big coolers in the bed of the truck. This is much more expensive than my little rig and draws much more power from the battery.

NETS

Nets used to catch bait have all been mentioned in the previous text. The most common is the cast net, followed by a haul seine and finally a gill net. Each state has different laws regarding the use of these nets, and local regulations must be checked before putting any one of them in the water.

For example, in Virginia a commercial license is required to catch food fish with a cast net. Sounds simple enough; you just want to catch bait. The Catch-22 is that spot, croaker, bluefish and several other species likely to show up in a cast net are considered food fish no matter how small. Because of this law and the way it is written, serious bait catchers purchase a cast-net license.

Most states have a recreational gill net law that allows a short net to be used by non-commercial fishermen. Some states still require a license to set this net while others do not. All require special markings to designate the net as recreational. And so it goes.

The haul seine also requires a license in some jurisdictions and not in others. The length and mesh size are the determining factors when a license is required.

It is also illegal to use a net in some locations. In Delaware a cast net may not be used within 300 feet of a spillway. This prevents the taking of large numbers of shad and herring in the spring. In addition, Delaware has passed a law prohibiting the possession of more than 10 herring in an effort to stop the trade in these fish as striper bait.

FOUL WEATHER GEAR

While every fisherman should have a good set of foul weather gear the bait fishermen will need them even when the weather is fair.

Bait fishing can be a messy game. Cutting up several flats of butter-fish or busting open a couple bushels of clams can cause the deposit of what the scientific community calls mung on the outer apparel of the person doing the work. Since these jobs are usually done at the beginning of a trip, it is a good idea if that outer apparel is something that can be cleaned off with a hose.

I have had a few pairs of foul weather gear over the years and currently own a set of Grundens. The bib overalls cover most of my body and will keep me reasonably clean while doing dirty jobs. The top is a pullover with elastic in the sleeves and can keep out the most determined water in the nastiest weather.

A high quality pair of pull-on boots will complete the outfit. I carry all of my foul weather gear in a plastic lined, waterproof duffle bag. The bag also contains my fishing gloves, a few dry towels and a clean pair of socks.

6

KNOTS FOR BAIT FISHING

IMPROVED CLINCH KNOT

Use this knot to attach a hook or snap to the leader, or a swivel to the main fishing line.

1. Pass the line through the eye of the hook, snap, or lure, then double it back and make five turns around the standing line. Hold the coils in place, and push the tag end through the first loop next to the eye, and then through the large loop.
2. Lubricate with saliva and draw the knot tight, being sure the coils do not overlap one another.

UNI-KNOT

The uni-knot is an excellent knot to use when attaching terminal tackle. This knot delivers up to 99 percent of the breaking strength of the unknotted line.

Before the coils slide down the line to jam against the eye of the lure or snap, wet the line so it is properly lubricated.

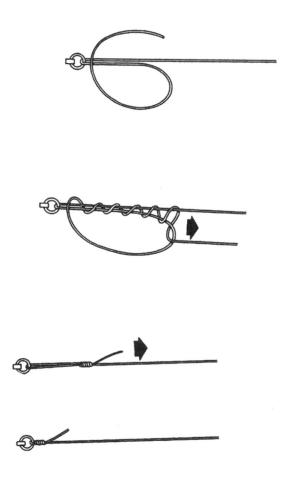

ALBRIGHT KNOT

This is the best knot to use to join a heavy leader to light line.

1. Double back a few inches of the heavy line (or wire) and pass about ten inches of the lighter line through the loop.

2. Wrap the light line back over itself and both strands of the heavy line. This is a bit easier if you hold the light line and both leader strands with your left thumb and forefinger, and wind with your right hand.

3. Make ten snug, neat wraps then pass the end of the line back through the original big loop, as shown.

4. While holding the coils in place, pull gently on both strands of the heavy line, causing the coils to move toward the end of the loop. Take out the slack by pulling on both strands of light line. When the knot is snug pull hard on the main light line and main heavy line. Pull as hard as you can for a good solid knot. Clip both excess tag ends close.

SURGEON'S KNOT

Use this knot when joining two lines of significantly different diameters.

1. Lay the line and leader parallel with an overlap of about eight inches.

2. Treat the two lines as a single line and tie an overhand knot, passing the entire leader through the loop. Leave the loop open.

3. Make a second overhand knot, again passing the whole leader and overlapped line through.

4. Hold both overlaps and pull in opposite directions to make the knot. Then pull the line only against the leader to set the knot. Clip the surplus ends close to the knot.

BLOOD KNOT

Use this knot to join two monofilament lines of similar diameters.

1. Overlap the two parallel lines by 12 inches total. Take five wraps on one side and pull the end back through between the two strands.
2. Repeat on the other side, pulling the other end through the strands in the opposite direction.
3. Pull the two tag ends slowly to gather the knot.
4. Once gathered neatly, pull the standing line to tighten the knot. Trim the tag ends.

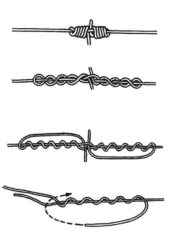

PERFECTION LOOP

The Perfection loop puts a loop in the end of a leader. The advantage of the Perfection loop is that the resulting loop always lays in line with the standing part of the leader—important for good presentation.

1. Place the tag end behind the standing part of leader, keeping the tag end on the right side.
2. Bring the tag end in from of the first loop and then wrap it behind the first loop, forming a new, smaller loop. Hold both loops in place with the left hand. Again the tag end is on the right. Place the tag end between the loops.
3. Pull the second loop through the first loop, lubricate and tighten by pulling on the second loop and the standing part of leader, and trim tag end.

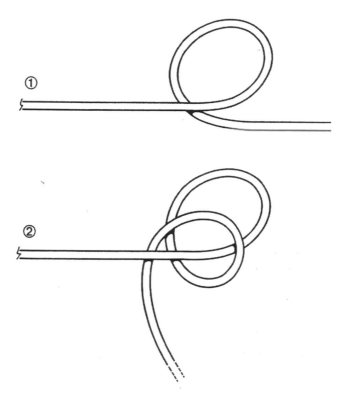

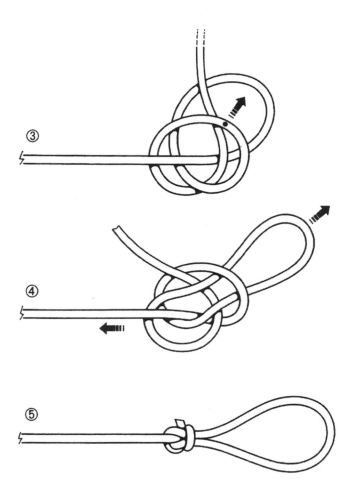

Index